Nubian Queen Self-Love

Black Women Cultivating Self-Care and Acceptance with Affirmations and a Growth Mindset

i

E-Book ISBN: 979-8-9865333-6-0

Paperback book ISBN: 978-1-959828-08-2

Hardcover book ISBN: 978-1-959828-16-7

DEDICATION

This compilation is a love letter to my Nubian Queen Sistas! I see you.

You are the backbone of all things the world holds dear. As the mother of humanity, you bear its worldly sorrows on your shoulders.

Do not despair for this burden is not yours to carry. Your only duty is to care for and love yourself.

ACKNOWLEDGMENTS

I wish to thank my husband, child, siblings, parents, aunties, uncles, cousins, and extended community for your support.

As for friends and colleagues, Claudette H, Donna G, Janet H, Leasa A, and the Shining Stars Mastermind Group – thanks to you for your reviews, edits, and encouragement.

Lastly, I thank Rosemarie P for her exceptional editing eye.

HOW TO USE THIS BOOK

Anything worth doing is worth starting poorly!

I repeat…

Anything worth doing is worth starting poorly!

I was brought up hearing the exact opposite! But if you consider a baby learning to talk or walk, the initial stages are filled with what we adults may perceive as "failures," when in fact, they are just learning experiences.

I hope you can appreciate that this journey on which we shall embark in this book is such an endeavor. We won't get everything perfectly right the first few times. So, please stay the course and I promise you that the person (you) who completes this path will love and accept herself!

There is a workbook sold with this book in which you can write down the answers to the exercises whether you read the e-book, paperback, or listen to the audiobook. I encourage you to sneak time from your busy days to write in the workbook. I hope this book is more than a read or hear now and forget the next minute experience. These exercises are fundamental to creating the shift we all need. Please do the exercises once, twice — or as many times as your need. Grab some friends and step through a chapter together. Then, rinse and repeat....

While undertaking this self-growth expedition, please can you share any breakthrough or suggestion?

TABLE OF CONTENTS

INTRODUCTION

"Always put on your oxygen mask before helping others."

- Any Airline

My fellow Black women, let's embark on a self-love journey! All I ask is that you put on your oxygen mask first before helping anyone else.

Women of color unjustly face racism and sexism in America and the rest of the world. That said, racism and sexism harm our physical and mental health in numerous ways. Racism commingled with sexism cause sadness, anxiety, and mental suffering. Consequently, Black women are more prone to pregnancy-related mortality, high blood pressure, heart disease, incarceration, and relationship violence. Societal racist and sexist microaggressions drain energy, leaving us barely able to meet societal obligations much less practice self-care. Embodying the depiction of a "strong Black woman" would oblige us to carry on despite being fatigued or ill. Others demand that we be strong for them every day, yet we are only human. We strive for excellence, but sometimes our greatest strength resides in knowing when to rest and self-care.

I am a Jamaican-born Black woman who has experienced racial and sexist microaggressions firsthand. Still, I want to inspire Black women and our future generations to love themselves unconditionally without needing society's approval. However, there is no way to be a hero if you do not care for yourself.

In writing this book, I provide a unique viewpoint in which you emphasize yourself — your self-care and self-love. Self-care means treating yourself well and making yourself a priority because you are a

Nubian Queen! Self-care is your birthright. You don't need anyone's approval. As Black women, we were taught that taking time for yourself is selfish. Like any other human being, you must maintain your mental and physical health. Luckily, you will discover the essentials of doing so in this manuscript.

I know self-love can be challenging. When we are taught to support everyone else, self-love can be viewed as selfish. Hence, I will explain self-love in the first chapter to shift your perspective. I am confident this book will open your mind to new ideas.

These chapters teach self-care essential tools and how to incorporate them into your hectic daily life. I explain the power of positive affirmations. Then, this text will introduce you to your inner child and adultification bias. From these concepts, I will share practical methods to safeguard your mental health, so self-care becomes routine. I'll link the growth mindset construct to your self-care and self-love.

Physically, Black women come in all sizes. Our body image is not a product of misguided media messages. However, we are still obligated to prioritize our health and fitness despite society's body shaming. This book teaches you how to improve your body image and health. Finally, embracing our unique spirituality and self-acceptance is essential to self-love. As a Black girl and now a single Black parent, I've had similar experiences as you and many women of color. So, you may trust my guidance on this journey to self-acceptance and self-love.

Since I was a little girl, I have known and believed that Black women are more resilient than any lie told about us, or any weapon used against us. We bring about change. We are dope Nubian Queens!

This book will make you a better person. After reading or listening to these words, you'll love yourself more and encourage other Black women to do the same. For your own health and well-being, I urge you to start this self-care journey. Prepare for a life-changing odyssey, my fellow Nubian Queen! Once your pilgrimage is underway, your regal self will emerge.

CHAPTER 1: Self-Love & the Black Woman

*"The most disrespected person in America
is a Black woman.
The most unprotected person in America
is a Black woman.
The most neglected person in America
is a Black woman."*

- Malcolm X

Malcolm X uttered the above remarks over 60 years ago on May 22, 1962! Unfortunately, his words are still true today as supported by numerous statistics that will be presented later in this book. Even though American society still does not appear to value Black women, we can learn to value ourselves. The ultimate step in the journey of valuing ourselves in defiance of society is self-love. Throughout this book, we'll explore how you can integrate self-care practices into your everyday life to achieve self-love because, my esteemed Nubian Queen…you are worth it! However, just before we dive into the intricacies of this concept, why don't we take some time to fully understand what it means?

The True Meaning of Self-Love

To explain self-love, I use a parenting example. I am a single mother, and trust me, there are times when I get upset by what my child does. But does that mean I don't love them? Of course not! Likewise, self-love doesn't imply always having positive feelings about yourself. There will be times when you are frustrated, angry, or even disappointed in yourself. In this case, self-love encompasses how you respond to these potentially demoralizing feelings. Moreover, self-love includes developing a hard shell against the comments of others. Self-love requires developing a higher self-esteem and valuing your opinions about yourself above the views of others. Honey, you are a kind soul, and self-love is reserving some of this kindness for yourself (*Martin, 2019*).

And yes, there's a difference between having self-love and being narcissistic or selfish. Narcissists lack empathy; they put themselves on a pedestal and believe they are better than everyone else. However, narcissists continually demand external validation to feel good about themselves. The belief in superiority must be fed by external confirmation. However, self-love is the direct opposite of being a narcissist. You aren't showing off how great you are when you love yourself. Instead, self-love means being honest about your insufficiencies and still choosing to care for yourself, regardless. My Nubian Queen, you are a bright, shining light! So, rather than being an act of selfishness, self-love entails making a conscious decision to preserve that beaming light while being surrounded by the darkness of disrespect and neglect.

Self-Love for the Black Woman

Why is the practice of self-love essential for Black women? Well, because we are entitled to it. Do you know that as of 2020, although Black girls and women make up about 14 percent of the youth population, they comprise one-third of the girls and women detained in the juvenile system? Are you aware that Black women earn less than their counterparts in the workplace? For example, the average Black woman in the workforce makes 63 cents for every $1 a White, non-Hispanic man earns in the U.S. (*Eltahir, 2022*).

And this reality is not due to lack of education. In fact, Black women currently make up one of the most educated cohorts in America. Still, those of us with advanced degrees earn less than White men with just a 2-year or 4-year college degree. Also, working Black women frequently are single mothers without a supporting legal spouse.

Do you know that although Black women have high career ambitions, they are less likely to find a mentor than their counterparts? Amid all these, we still must handle several forms of sexual harassment. Every day, we deal with a constant barrage of microaggressions, which cast doubt about our competence, skill, and intelligence.

Basically, racism and sexism can suffocate us if we let them. Aside from the emotional trauma that accompanies the daily doses of racism that we receive as we inhabit the world each day, there are also biological consequences. For example, according to the Study of Women's Health Across the Nation, Black women are 7.5 years biologically older than White women — mainly due to additional trauma we endure (*Eltahir, 2022*).

I don't know about you, but these statistics are exasperating. And, you know the most annoying part? We can't change our exposure to these daily external microaggressions affecting our lives. As Victor Frankl stated in *Man's Search for Meaning*, "When we are no longer able to change a situation, we are challenged to change ourselves." While we may not control these actions directed at us, we can focus on what is within our control.

And here's where self-love comes in. Society oppresses us in countless ways with daily microaggressions. Let's not direct our energy at trying to change how people perceive or treat us. The highest form of protest is not an outward show of grievances. Instead, it is an inward appreciation of our value. Fittingly, practicing self-love redirects our energy toward changing how we treat ourselves—and how we treat all our fellow *Self-Loving Soul Sistas.*

In other words, self-love isn't a feeling—it's a choice. And it begins with understanding our worth. I'll cover how you can accept yourself for who you are later in this book, but may I take a moment now to tell you that, girl, you are "*a woman on fiyah!*" The world can try to snuff out your light, but I don't want you to allow it to happen. Just so you know, you are worth every bit of energy you expend on yourself. That leads me to ask one question.

How Much Self-Love Are You Giving?

From what I've said so far, you must understand how important self-love is, especially for us women of the *melanated* clan. And it only makes sense to take an honest evaluation of where we stand before moving forward. This is true because progress in any endeavor is directly proportional to an awareness of what ground needs to be traversed.

Below is a list of questions that can measure how much you love yourself (*Walker, 2022*). Just like in any assessment, this exercise's value is commensurate with how honest about yourself you're willing to be. For any statement below, please answer either "*Yes*," "*No*," or "*Sometimes*."

- For every "Yes," give yourself a 2.
- For every "Sometimes," add a 1 to your score, and
- For every "No," you get 0 point. Clear?

Okay, let's go! Remember, don't answer these questions based on what you think they should be; choose your answers based on your ***current*** reality. Ready? Here we go.

1.   Every time I look in the mirror, I feel good about myself.

2.   I'm comfortable in my own skin when I step into a room.

3. Although I make mistakes, I quickly forgive myself and move on.

4. Whenever people criticize me, I don't take it too personally. Instead, I accept the feedback, examine it, and improve myself based on it.

5. I'm convinced I'm a lovable person.

6. When I feel tired or stressed, I deny requests from others. I simply say "no."

7. I know that it's normal to feel down at times. But I find positive ways to brighten my mood whenever I feel an undesirable emotion.

8. I recognize my imperfections and accept them entirely.

9. I trust my decisions.

10. Things don't always go according to plan. Still, I'm kind to myself in these times.

11. People are lucky to have me in their lives; I add value to anyone around me.

12. Regardless of the situation, I do what is best for my mental and physical health.

13. My opinion matters.

14. When I am around people, I find it easy to be myself.

Now, it is time to add up your score. What did you get? Since you truthfully answered the questions, here is an appraisal of where you currently stand on this self-love journey.

- If your score falls between 21 - 28, you are *Self-Love Savvy*! You have come a long way in integrating acts of self-love into your routine, demonstrating your love for yourself. However, remember that self-love isn't a one-time thing. Instead, it is an ongoing process that will prove valuable when life gets challenging. So, keep reading to elevate your mastery of self-love even more.

- If your score is between 14 - 20, you are doing well. I would call you *Self-Love Smart.* Although you know self-love's importance, you have not yet successfully introduced all the necessary vital aspects. That is fine. Since you have already begun this journey, let us keep the momentum going. Also, take note of questions where you answered "no" or "sometimes." For example, do you find yourself shrinking in fear when you step into a room full of unknown faces? Maybe it is time to work on your confidence. Or, on the other hand, are you having a hard time saying no? Perhaps it is time to fine tune specific self-love skills!

- If you find yourself with score between 0 -13, that is okay! In fact, I am excited that you are reading this book. I have specifically crafted this book for the *Self-Love Seeker* like you. So that you are aware, many people fall into this category. Now that we all know where you land, I assure you that picking up this book might be your best decision this year. Let's learn how you can make self-love a priority on your list.

Making Small Acts of Self-Love a Priority

The famous Chinese proverb says that a journey of a thousand miles begins with a single step. This passage to being an unapologetic, resolved, consummate self-lover starts with small actions of self-love each day. In a bit, I will list a few activities for building up your self-love muscles. However, all of that will be mere empty gestures unless you recognize one crucial detail: your worth.

So, let's begin with worthiness. Everything we do is a statement of who we are. If you regard yourself highly, chances are you will do things that demonstrate this positive perception of yourself. When you wake up in the morning without makeup, are you scared to look in your eyes? Do you feel a crippling anxiety when it's time to look in the mirror? Do you like what you see? If you don't, that's fine. But from today forward, this recoil ends. Today marks the day when you start loving yourself and your reflected physical image.

Go grab a pen and paper or your workbook. Now, write down everything you love about yourself. Is it those eyes others frequently admired or the smile you've constantly gotten compliments about? Is it your kindness toward those around you or your unearthly patience? Whatever it is, write it down. Then, keep going until you generate a healthy list of more than 7 non-duplicated items. I must point something out at this juncture: regardless of how important self-love is, it could be challenging to practice it in an unsupportive environment like the one we Black women so often inhabit.

If you find negative thoughts sneaking into your mind as you carry out this exercise, don't worry. We will soon learn how to overcome this habit. Just observe those unproductive thoughts as they come, let them go, and focus on turning to the good! In the beginning it might feel slightly uncomfortable to compliment yourself because you are not used to being your own cheerleader, but if you continue to do this, the self-love words will feel more natural.

Once you finish listing the things you love about yourself, step in front of a mirror. Then, say "hi" to your reflection, and proceed to give you — that Nubian Queen in the mirror — a long, relaxed gaze. Then, read out (aloud) the list of things you love about yourself. Repeat it 2 or 3 times, and you will be closer to fully accepting yourself despite your perceived shortcomings. Make this a daily habit. Now let's talk about down-to-earth ways you could practice self-love in your daily undertakings *(Les @ Balanced Black Girl, 2017)*.

Be Present

Let's be honest with each other — life is full of distractions. Whether it is an email notifying you of a new task or trending news on social media, it is too easy to get caught up in the "motion of life." However, self-love begins with choosing to spend time with yourself. Think about it. Do you remember how you longed to spend time with your first crush? The thrills and emotions came with just being with your loved one. The same idea applies here. As a show of how much you love yourself, start spending time doing what *you* love doing. This could mean painting, meditating, journaling, writing, or watching your favorite show or movie. Whatever your personal self-love act is, ensure you are present. Create a distraction-free zone by turning off your notifications or putting your phone on airplane mode.

Recognize and Accept Your Uniqueness

Everyone has a bit of eccentricity in their body composition, such as freckles, dimples, or pigeon toes. These are the aspects that make each human being unique out of billions of people. This could manifest as a hobby you are crazy about, but others may consider mundane. Or better yet, an uncommon craving you have, that others can't just seem to understand. Whatever it is, embrace your nuttiness. That is what makes you, you. And, if you'll truly love yourself, begin by understanding that perfection is a façade.

Be Intentional About What You Consume

Self-love isn't simply an emotional affair. It could also have a physical component. What you put into your body is very important. If you keep consuming junk all the time, you may want to ask yourself if you truly value yourself. Instead, nourish yourself with nutritional foods. Don't forget to drink lots of water. That Nubian skin has got to glow!

Take in Positive Words

Try not to combat negative thoughts with positive thoughts. Instead, do so using positive comments. Begin by scanning what words you are exposed to daily — the lyrics in the music you hear, what your friends tell you, and your self-talk. Do all of these reflect positivity? If so, great. If not, it's time to make an adjustment. When you look in the mirror, admit how beautiful you are. Whenever you respond with kindness to a racist or refuse to be defined by society's limits, do not consider such actions "normal." Instead, give yourself a pat on the back with your encouraging words.

Learn to Say "No"

I cannot overemphasize how important this small practice can be for your mental and physical well-being. In a world where a lot of our tasks can be done over the internet, drawing a line between our work and personal lives may be difficult— especially if you are a workaholic. Even more, society expects us to be "strong Black women," forgetting that we are not superheroes and are deserving of rest.

There is so much to do! Society demands so much of us women, plus, as a Black woman, you continually put in twice the effort to prove you are as good as your colleagues. This can lead to poor work-life balance and little time for self-care. Moreover, we run households, church committees, care for our children and other relatives. We become exhausted and chronically in short supply of sleep and time for self-care.

A significant part of self-care is accepting that you are worthy of self-love and your time. Once you acknowledge this, the next step is learning to assertively say "no". Unless you consciously guard your time, people will steal it without remorse. Here are a few tips to help you say "no" when the need arises:

- Use visual cues. Let what you say to be consistent with your body language. Of course, you don't need to pierce the requester with a long stare but making occasional eye contact as you respond conveys the message more effectively.
- To prevent the feelings of guilt that come with saying "no", suggest alternatives to the person making the request. Such options could be scheduling the job at hand for a later date or recommending someone else to handle the task.
- Avoid long excuses and justifications. When people see that you are too apologetic about your refusal, they know that they can easily massage your "no" into a "yes." Let your response be brief and concise.

Hence, people will want you to go out of your way to help them, often at the cost of your mental and physical health. However, learning to say no will help you avert the overwhelming mountain of a task. So, do not beat around the bush. Although we must say it politely, just say it, Nubian Queen. A tip to doing so without qualms of guilt is suggesting another option to the asker.

Amid all these, a holistic approach to self-love requires the integration of emotional self-care. So, if you currently ignore your emotions, it's time you face those suppressed feelings.

CHAPTER 2: Integrating Self-Care

C hapter 1 introduced us to how important it is for Black women to love themselves. This chapter address a critical component of self-love—self-care.

As 6 children being raised by a single mom, we never went on any vacation – ever! However, every year we would visit our mom in the hospital. Like clockwork, she would be hospitalized for conditions, which I now understand were related to exhaustion and fatigue. You see, the terms of her divorce from our father was no alimony and the

bare minimum in child support for his 6 children –
which Dad skipped out on paying.

Consequently, as a result of her grim situation,
mom worked 3 jobs! In her absence, my sister and I
became the surrogate cooks and house keepers.
Year after year of working 3 jobs to feed here 6
children took a toll on my mom's health. Her
"vacations" were those hospital stays as her health
declined from the burden she carried. I have a
couple traumatized siblings who absolutely refuse
to go to any hospital for any reason – even for
something a trivial as visiting a sick relative or
friend.

Accordingly, my late mother was that "strong
Black woman!" More importantly, she was the
poster child of that Black woman who could not
afford - in dollars or time, to practice any self-care.
My late mother's memory is a huge motivation for
writing this book.

Dire Consequences of Lack of Self-Care

On January 30, 2020, Cheslie leaped from her apartment roof top to her death. By age 30, Cheslie was accomplished. She was the North Carolina attorney who fought for social justice and criminal justice reform. Not just that, she was also an Emmy-nominated TV show correspondent and a former Miss USA. But, amidst all of this, behind the veil of her beautiful smile hid the monster of depression (*Jagoo, 2022*). I wish someone had told the deceased former Miss USA, Cheslie Kryst that she did not have to be a "strong Black woman."

I can't help but imagine what would have happened to Chelsie if we, as a society, encouraged each other to pay attention to our emotions. What if we Black women became more engaged about giving our mental health the care it deserves? What if we decided it was acceptable to not be "strong"? This is what I want to discuss in this chapter. I want to show you what life would look like if you are not expected to play the "strong Black woman" role in society.

What if we Black women became more engaged about giving our health the care it deserves? What if we decided it was acceptable to not be "strong"? This is what I want to discuss in this chapter. I want to show you what life would look like if you are not expected to play the "strong Black woman" role in society.

What Does Emotional Self-Care Look Like?

When you need to take a day off from work, how do you react? Do you reproach yourself for being selfish? After all, you have friends who need your time, kids who need your attention, a "significant other" who needs love, and a host of other responsibilities you shouldn't be ignoring, right?

From the outside, self-care can appear selfish. But are you truly being selfish? Let's examine how to overcome this limiting belief, or else, engaging in constant self-care will be impossible.

As Black women, we've been trained by society to do for others before ourselves. This is the only perspective on life we've known. We have seen our mothers embody the essence of strong women all their lives. They never shirked their responsibilities. So, it becomes a learned behavior at their feet—to endure despite the hardships, when in fact we are just as human as everyone. We are in as much need of self-care as anyone else. That is not being a weakling; it is being human. And, until you absorb this concept of our basic human need, it is difficult to practice self-care without guilt.

In fact, coming to terms with our need for self-care is the greatest act of strength we can display to our children and to every other woman of color in our sphere of influence. To Black women, self-care must not be construed as an act of selfishness. Instead, it is an undoing of the generational trauma we were bequeathed. Black woman self-care is a change in the status quo and a reminder that we have human needs.

In other words, if your obligations include taking care of others, you must begin by taking care of yourself. Or, of what use is a light if it cannot shine to its full potential? Often, the burdens from society dim our lights. So, the first step to restoring ourselves is admitting we need recharging and are worthy of self-care.

Hence, emotional self-care is more about ensuring you don't suppress your feelings at the expense of being "strong." Emotional self-care is more about going through rather than getting over the emotions inside of us. Emotional self-care involves consciously processing your emotions, thoughts, and feelings about ordeals you previously endured or currently face. Surely, that's not an easy task to accomplish, but coming to terms with our emotions is a skill we must all master to self-care.

To get comfortable with your emotions, let's begin with the basics. Emotions are normal. Rather than labeling the emotions you feel as "good" or "bad," see your emotions as messages sent by your body to tell you how a situation or event makes you feel (*Scott, 2022*). Although these emotions come in different forms, feelings of happiness, joy, and peace are positive. In contrast, other emotions are labeled as negative, such as feelings of anger, frustration, and fear. Either way, since every feeling on the emotional spectrum is a message, let's focus on the "message" rather than focusing on a label.

Emotions help us pay more attention to the events and what caused them. Our reaction to these emotions is more important than how they make us feel. For instance, a woman could make a career-wrecking decision out of happiness, thus leading to a job loss. In contrast, another woman could set appropriate boundaries in her relationships out of anger, leading to healthier friendships. In this case, though happiness is labeled as positive and anger as negative; it is the reaction of the affected individual that determines consequences—not the type of emotion. This is what is meant by "managing" your emotions.

However, this concept of emotion management is not that simple. While you don't want to avoid your emotions, you shouldn't allow these emotions to wreak havoc on your day, mood, and, ultimately, your physical health. Therefore, learning to create balance in your emotional health through emotional self-care is important. Emotional self-care also means trusting our emotions and intuition. Emotions perceived from the causative events are just responses to external stimuli.

The feelings help us understand how to react to the stimuli. In this case, you should first embrace the fact that you feel that way. Second, determine the exact source of the feeling, and then act accordingly with maturity. An overreaction from a place of immaturity can be problematic. In other words, getting comfortable with your emotions means understanding how you feel and accepting the feeling. Then seek healthy ways to respond to a situation. This mature pattern of behavior begins by becoming more emotionally aware.

Techniques to Become More Emotionally Aware

The first step to becoming emotionally aware is being in the present (*Emotional Intelligence Toolkit*). This means becoming mindful of the sensations your mind tuned out to ignore your emotions. You can do this by carrying out a "grounding" exercise.

This exercise employs the use of your sense organs to bring you into the present.

What Can You See?

Sure, you've got eyes, but what can you observe around you? Take a moment to look around: observe the flowers as they sway to the music of the wind, your mirror as it shows you how beautiful you are, and your wardrobe as it houses your best clothes. Locate and notice about 5 of these objects in your surroundings.

What Can You Touch?

Get the sensation that comes from physical contact with your body. Without moving an inch, come to terms with the signals your body is sending you from the items you presently contact. It could be your cell phone as it balances carefully within your palm or the chair you sit on as it gallantly keeps you away from the ground. Feel 4 of these touch items. If you are not presently in contact with up to 4 items, gently move your body around until you've felt more objects around you.

Can You Hear Any Sound?

The mind has a way of allowing you to get used to constant sounds after a while. Reverse this process and get in tune with the sounds your environment is producing. It could be the chirping of some nearby birds or the sounds of the gentle breeze that blows past your face. Hear 3 of these sounds again.

What Can You Smell?

Check out your surroundings, looking out for fragrances that are worth smelling. Once you perceive 2 of these of these smells, move on to the final step.

Identify One Thing You Can Taste

It could be a scoop of ice cream, a sachet of mint, or a sip of water. Whatever it is, feel the delight your tongue brings as it reveals the true nature of the food item.

That's it, the whole grounding exercise. Whenever you feel out of touch with your emotions and you want to become more conscious of how you feel, the first step is to take a step back and mentally remove yourself from the source of stress. Once you've become more aware of your surroundings, you then become further capable of observing your emotions from a third-person's lens. Also, you become capable of making more profound decisions with the information your emotions feed you. In this state, you can take the following steps:

Give the Feeling a Name

It comes as a feeling, but it should not end there.
Give the emotion a name. I'm not talking about the
easy names such as anger, fear, or frustration; I am
referring to more specific names that can only come
from digging deeper into the core of your
emotional being. You might say you feel sad, when
actually you feel vulnerable and victimized. Or you
might identify anger, when in fact you feel
humiliated and disrespected. When you become
more specific in naming how you feel, you can then
come to terms with the "why." (*Bergen, 2016*).
Hence, it becomes easier to proffer a solution to the
feeling. To help you with this exercise, please use
the *Feelings Wheel* (*McGill, 2022*) and on page 8 of
the workbook.

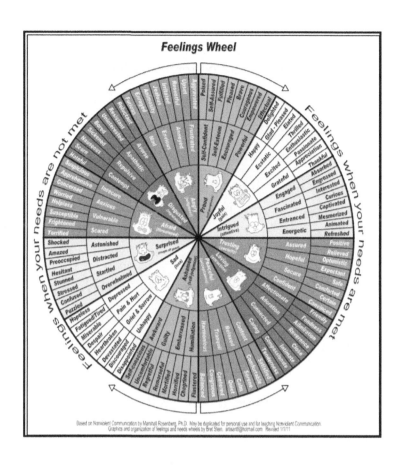

Based on Nonviolent Communication by Marshall Rosenberg, Ph.D. May be duplicated for personal use and for teaching Nonviolent Communication. Graphics and organization of feelings and needs wheels by Bret Stein. artisanfl@hotmail.com Revised 1/1/11

Track Your Feelings Throughout the Day

As I previously stated, our emotions are report cards of how specific events, which we can call "triggers," make us feel. Hence, to prevent certain emotions, such as those that bring more negativity than positivity, we had better avoid the triggers. Or better still, if the trigger is out of our control, we must learn to expect the emotions and devise a strategy for coping with them when they arise. To do this, pick a feeling for each day and follow through with that feeling throughout the day (*Bergen, 2016*).

For instance, let's pick "Happiness." Open a notepad on your phone or get a physical pen and paper. As you go through your daily activities, observe what made you happy. Was it when you felt valued and respected by a fellow co-worker or when you were inspired by another woman of color? What were you doing when you felt happy? Working on an exciting project or watching a peaceful movie? Whatever and whenever you have the feeling, document it.

Tracking and documenting a single emotion throughout the day help you ascertain for sure what your triggers are for certain feelings and aids you in becoming more emotionally intelligent. Take for example, an emotion that is on the more positive side of the spectrum, like happiness. You then know for sure what to do, whom to be with and where to go to feel happy. And for an emotion that tilts toward the more negative end of the spectrum, like anger, you know what triggers it. Then, you can easily carry out the next step.

Express Your Emotions in a Healthy Way

As I have previously said, emotions are not necessarily "good" or "bad." They reflect how we react to stimuli. When we feel emotions such as anger, sadness, or frustration, it is naive to attempt to bury them inside, hoping never to express or feel them again. It is tempting to try and run away from these emotions, but avoidance is not the useful way of managing our emotions. Instead, we need to learn to express our emotions in healthy ways. However, before doing so, let's begin by understanding the unhealthy ways of expressing our emotions.

I have stated one before - avoidance coping. This is when you avoid your emotions, pretending they don't exist and projecting a false exterior. For instance, if an assigned task at work gets you stressed out, a form of avoidance coping will be procrastinating on doing the job at hand. And while this might initially provide some sort of temporary relief, in the long run, as the deadline for the job approaches, you will inevitably tackle it under more intense stress. This time, the stress becomes mixed with anxiety. This also applies to other negatively inclined emotions such as anger and frustration.

My Nubian Queen, if a toxic relationship makes you feel angry and disrespected, skipping the hard conversations will only prolong the feelings of anger and disrespect. However, admitting how hurt you feel by the actions of the other party, although seemingly difficult at first, provides long-term relief. Aside from avoidance coping, other negative ways of dealing with your emotions are as follows.

Self-harm can be either via physical devices such as objects or mental devices such as self-destructive thoughts. Examples of self-destructive thoughts are ruminating and dwelling on negative feelings rather than acting on the information provided by such feelings. Another negative way of dealing with our emotions is *false positivity*, where we shame ourselves for experiencing negative emotions and force ourselves to appear more positive than we are.

On the other hand, there are positive ways of coping with negative emotions. By now, I hope that you can claim the emotions you feel and track the events that cause the emotions. A positive way of dealing with your emotions is changing the things you can. For instance, if a constant source of stress for you is the overwhelming workload, a great step would be communicating with your supervisor and, if possible, delegating tasks to others. In society, people see us Black women as being capable of doing the most strenuous tasks without flinching. But you don't have to fit into that narrative. If you are being overstressed, simply cut down the workload. You have that within your control.

Unfortunately, not everything can be within your control. One example is people's view of us. A positive way of dealing with things outside our control would be to avoid ruminating on what you cannot change. Other positive ways of managing your emotions include engaging in regular exercise, meditation, and finding ways to laugh more. All of these are healthy outlets for your emotions. We will cover most of these in detail as we move further in this book.

Pay Attention to Your Body

Our body is a wonderful communicator of our emotions, but how often do we listen to it? Do you recall the tingly feeling you felt in your stomach when you had your first crush? Or the anger that burned in your upper chest when someone tried body-shaming you? Or the breathlessness that held your guts when you had stage fright? All of these are ways our bodies tell us how we feel. However, the voice of the body is muted and easy to ignore. Pause for a minute and take stock. How do you feel right now? What is your body telling you?

Now, you are equipped with the weapons to fight your emotional warfare! I must point out that you may not become emotionally aware immediately. However, just as it takes years for a baby's bones to mature, as you continually practice these tips, your emotional awareness muscles will become more powerful.

The way I have laid out several points in this chapter, you might be tempted to believe all of these are easy to engage in, and unfortunately, for us Black women, they are not. If self-love and self-care were easy, Black women across the world would be thriving. The negativity that society constantly imparts and the subtle messages that we do not deserve any attention we give to ourselves could easily get in the way of our engagement in these positive self-care practices. What if I told you that you could cut the societal ropes of negativity that have held you bound by simply listening to your inner child?

CHAPTER 3: Healing Your Inner Child

"We readily feel for the suffering child, but cannot see the child in the adult who, [her] soul fragmented and isolated..."

- Dr. Gabor Matè

T he first two chapters discussed the importance of self-love for Black women and how critical emotional self-care is. Now, let us turn to the concept of the "inner child" and healing her.

She was required to care for her younger and older siblings. Her brothers had free playtime while she cooked and cleaned. She was sexualized as a child or pre-teen. Right now, she lives deep inside you, fighting off experiencing those awful feelings again. She presents herself to the world in the forms of fear, anxiety, and perfectionism. All these portrayals are just her attempts to feel safe and in control. Allow me to introduce you to your inner child.

What Is the Inner Child?

Our inner child is the free-spirited part of us that looks at life through the innocent lens of a child. She experiences life as a child does. And while she holds the positive aspects of being a child — such as creativity, innocence, and joy — she also carries those wounds and hurts she has encountered over the years. Your inner child is the part of you from your younger years. Your inner child is the younger you. She is the "you" that was present when you were a baby, infant, and toddler.

She resides within your subconscious mind and can often recall past experiences such as childhood fears and trauma. You can view this "inner child" as a separate entity, a mystical being that most psychologists agree exists. Or is it best to see your inner child as the emotional embodiment of your past experiences, but this time with positive outcomes *(Goldstein, 2022)*?

We all have an inner child. For instance, do you remember when a sarcastic comment from a colleague threw you back to the moment you felt incompetent in elementary school because you failed a test? Or the moment you felt like crying when you walked past a shop and perceived a smell that reminded you of your mom's cooking? Or the instance you tried so hard to feel loved as a teenager because you spent years growing up in a broken family without affection? All those experiences were moments when your inner child spoke up. But we ignore this vulnerable, little being we all have within us because she can bring back painful memories. So perhaps it's high time we began listening to our inner child. Can you hear what she is trying to tell you?

Presently, you might feel stuck. You might be trying to make progress in a certain area of your life. But instead of moving forward, you find yourself being weighed down by an unseen force. This is one way in which your inner child might be trying to get in touch with you. She needs you to heal from your past trauma before moving on. In this case, the only way to move forward is to retrace your steps backward.

A major part of your emotional self-care goal should be to create a collaborative team with your inner child (*Goldstein, 2022*). Successful people—not necessarily people who are rich, but those who live a happy, peaceful, and fulfilled life—understand this. Just like how a team divided against itself cannot win a game, it will be difficult for you to win the game of life if a part of you—your inner self—keeps standing in your way. So, you must introduce your adult self to your inner child. Carry out the introduction with these two steps:

Begin a Dialogue, Say "Hi"

How do you begin a relationship with a new friend? First, you develop the intent to honestly know the person. In your first meeting, you don't spend the entire time talking about yourself, your achievement, or your failures. Instead, you pay rapt attention to what the person has to say. You notice the person's likes, hopes, dreams, fears, and pains. And slowly, as she learns that she can trust you, she leans into you, revealing more and more as the friendship deepens. The same principle applies to knowing your inner child.

You can decipher the intentions of your inner child by keeping an open mind. Begin with a deep longing within you to hear what she has to say. So, take a moment to calm your mind. Block out the usual conscious adult thoughts, you know, those ponderings about the approaching deadline for your work project and other life responsibilities. Just focus on your inner child.

After creating space for a conversation, take it a step further. Meditate on your curiosity to learn about your inner child. Remember, your inner child represents a revelation of your past experiences, including hopes, dreams, fears, and worries. This curiosity invites your inner child out of her hiding place. Finally, she can be heard. Finally, she can speak.

Listen

As you remain in this state of focus, thoughts will emerge. These thoughts would appear to be different from the ones you are used to. These thoughts will contain childlike fervor and innocent curiosity. Your thinking will fill with lost hopes and dreams long buried under the weight of societal expectations. Now that you've snapped out of the never-ending rhythm of life, you can give these dreams room to come alive again. You've created a space for them to be believed once more. You may begin to remember painful moments you never dealt with. The sharp pangs of your broken family may pierce through your heart once more, and the tears hidden behind the smile resurface. Suddenly you will realize that you've cracked the code — you can hear your inner child again.

Healing Your Inner Child - the Pathway to Recovery from Trauma

Now that we've covered a general approach to healing from trauma, let's take a closer look at one trauma common among Black women: the *adultification trauma*. Adultification trauma — otherwise known as adultification bias — is how society views Black girls as less innocent and more "mature" compared to their White counterparts. (5 *Effective Ways to Heal Your Inner Child from Adultification Trauma, 2021)*. This bias necessitates that Black girls grow up subjected to grueling standards and are given harsher treatments, leading to the assumption that Black girls are "used to it." This adultification preconception results in society not protecting Black girls. Furthermore, these girls are forced into prematurely dealing with the responsibilities of adulthood.

As a result, we grow into women who are less vocal about our emotions as we were saddled with "more important things." Rather than speak up about our needs, society subtly trains us to quietly tolerate this mistreatment and be "strong." We have been subconsciously trained to expect to be disregarded; it then becomes revolutionary to project confidence in our abilities. In other words, society does not wait until we are mature women before bestowing on us the "strong Black women" title. The "strong Black woman" message was embedded into our subconscious since we were children.

If you've been affected by this adultification bias, your inner child might still be dealing with the wound. You may not have realized how this was affecting you as a kid, and also now. Your inner child buried the pain and allowed you to keep growing through this dysfunctional society. While the emotional heartaches you feel might be a result of your inner child's weeping for attention, your best path to healing is through your inner child. Here is how you can deal with adultification trauma:

Listen to Your Inner Child

The first step to solving a problem is admitting there is a problem. To heal healthily, you must begin by acknowledging the injury. Accept as truth that the adultification trauma affected how you grew up. You are not shifting any blame on society for how you were affected. You are simply stating an uneasy fact. The adultification trauma caused us to become accustomed to not recognizing we've been hurt. And, ironically, to heal from this trauma, we need to admit we were indeed emotionally harmed. To accomplish healing, first, observe certain behavior traits in your life. These can be trust issues or the fear of speaking out when someone hurts you. Other manifestations can be dreading asking for help when you feel stuck or not being in touch with your emotions as you move through the day. Observe how these behaviors are linked to the childhood trauma you experienced.

Rediscover Yourself

Adultification trauma imposes certain labels that you may have embraced until now. What are these labels? For instance, some people uphold the label of Black women being "aggressive." So, when you challenge ideas or philosophies, people immediately conclude that you are the "angry Black woman." One would think that anger genes are intertwined within the DNA of the Black woman. It's time to rediscover yourself. Who are you? What other labels has society adhered to your being? For what cause would you like to advocate—even if this cause represents a well-accepted stereotype of Black women in your community? What do you enjoy doing that other Black women around you are afraid of embracing? Set some time aside to meet you—the inner you.

Write a Letter to Your Inner Child

By the time you are done with step 2, the inner child will have helped you unlock some possibilities in you that have been kept hidden for years. And now, just like what would happen in any conversation, it's time to send her a reply. You've got to do it the old fashion way. Grab a pen and paper and get ready to write a letter to your younger self (see page 13 of the *Nubian Queen Self-Love Workbook*). Begin by choosing an age or stage of your life you want to focus on. Spend some time feeling how the younger you (of that age) would have felt and tell yourself what you wished you had been told as a child.

Allow the old you to take the role of the parent and the younger you, a child. Be open; consistently validate the feelings of the younger you while dismissing the societal opinions that had held you bound. Tell your inner child you are sorry for yielding to the pressures you faced and promise to live a life free of the influence of society. End the letter by telling your inner child how much you love her. Then, make a vow to be you going forth.

Practice Being You

Let's review how far you've come. You began by admitting how the adultification bias has affected you. Then, you went on to invite your inner child to reintroduce you to yourself. Finally, you wrote a letter to your inner child, vowing to live for yourself. Now, it is time to fulfill that commitment.

Engage in radical self-care. Yes, you've got responsibilities, but still, you are not a tough human void of emotions. You are a Nubian Queen, girl! Set healthy work boundaries and enjoy your own company. Create time to go have fun with fellow Nubian Queens and make your joy something worth fighting for! Relieve yourself of any societal pressure and practice being you!

Don't Forget to Take Care of Your Inner Child

You may have wants that your inner child didn't receive, whether emotional or material. As you pay attention to being radical about your self-care, try satisfying those desires that were not fulfilled when you were a kid. This is how you can have regular contact with your inner child. But there are other ways of doing so.

How to Keep in Touch with Your Inner Child

Now, that you've begun the process of healing, it would be unwise to lose touch with your inner child. It is a good idea to make sure this newly developed relationship remains intact so that it's not so easy to fall into the previous traps and mistakes with mental health. Here are tips to keep building a relationship with your inner child:

- What were your hobbies as a kid? Painting? Solving a puzzle? Playing an instrument? Think back to when you were a kid, figure out what you loved doing, and find a way to integrate it into your schedule.

- Get back into the water. If you have kids, engage in water fights with them. The cool touch of water on your skin has a way of awakening your inner child.

- Get used to talking to her. While you fix your face in the mirror, say hello to your inner child. Ask how she's doing. On your day off, ask her what she would like to do. When you regularly pay attention to your inner child, it becomes easier to recognize when something's wrong and act appropriately. Remember, every successful person has a healthy inner child!

We just explored how you can connect with your inner child. Now it's time to give her positivity in the form of affirmations.

CHAPTER 4: *The Power of Positive Affirmations*

"Your mind will always believe everything you tell it. Feed it faith. Feed it truth. Feed it with love."

– Anonymous

O ur inner child appeared in the previous chapter. So, considering your newfound ability to communicate with her, it is time to replace negative words with encouraging expressions. Positive affirmations are such thoughts that we can start practicing now.

What Are Affirmations, and How Do They Work?

It is estimated that we humans have about 50,000 thoughts every day. And out of these, about 70-80% are estimated to be negative (*Lambersky, 2013*).

Oftentimes, we have these thoughts subconsciously; we don't want them, but we just find ourselves "having" them. The problem with this is that any repeated action leads to mastery. Frequent repetition of negative thoughts in our minds causes these thoughts to master us. And when they do, they find their way into our actions, then our behaviors, and eventually, our character.

Thoughts are powerful, and the best way to change certain traits about yourself is to change the mindset sponsoring the trait. Really, our physical lives are merely manifestations of our mental state. We subconsciously base our actions on our thoughts. Hence, when these thoughts are not self-serving, making poor decisions is the usual outcomes. Each thought leads to the phenomenon psychologists call "self-fulfilling prophecy."

A self-fulfilling prophecy occurs when an originally false social belief causes a person to act in ways to justify that false belief. For instance, if a lady has no belief in her qualifications to be a top leader of a multi-million-dollar company, chances are she will act in ways that will keep her away from such a position. So, if she has an interview that will potentially give her that position, she becomes anxious because of her false expectation or beliefs. Due to her anxiety, she is unable to provide the interviewer with any evidence of her competence. Consequently, the anxiety-prone performance prevents her from getting the top job. It is important that we refrain from these damaging thoughts before they become our reality. And, in this fight is where positive affirmations arise.

Affirmations are positive statements that replace the negative thoughts that have gained dominance in our minds over the years. Rather than viewing affirmations as "unrealistic thinking," see them instead as a mental exercise. Just like how physical exercises cause you to stay physically fit, mental exercises such as positive affirmations help you remain mentally and emotionally fit. Furthermore, science supports the use of affirmations. It has been proven that affirmations help you perform better at work. For instance, going over your top work qualities before high pressure meetings such as performance interviews, can help calm your nerves and significantly increase your chance of doing well. Again, research shows that positive affirmations can be used to treat mental health conditions such as low self-esteem and depression *(Using Affirmations: Harnessing Positive Thinking, 2022)*. That said, here are some affirmations to kickstart your journey into positive thinking.

Inspirational Affirmations for Black Women

5 Examples for Wellness

1. My play is as important as my work.
2. I am committed to taking care of myself.

3. Rest is on top of my priority list.

4. I am human, and I try to be one.

5. I say no whenever a proposed deadline is too close.

5 Examples for Self-Love & Confidence

1. I speak up against what hurts me; I value my voice.

2. I love myself completely and fully.

3. I do what brings me joy and peace.

4. I show up as my authentic self every single day.

5. Love flows through me. Love resides in me.

5 Examples for Meeting Goals & Motivation

1. I appreciate the small steps I take every day.

2. All things are working in my favor.

3. I love the woman I am becoming.

4. I can do great things.

5. How far I can reach depends solely on me.

5 Examples for Healthy Relationships

1. I find people who love me unconditionally.

2. I belong to a society of vibrant Black women.

3. I draw strength from others around me.

4. I am strong when I ask for help.

5. My love for myself helps me love others.

5 Examples for Conquering Fear

1. I feel fear but don't let it stop me from doing what I must anyway.

2. I walk in peace, knowing that I can do everything.

3. Only my present and future define me.

4. I choose to let go of the fear that holds me back.

5. I walk with confidence into the life I deserve.

5 Examples for Money & Career

1. I am worthy of every good thing this world offers.

2. I define what I get to do.

3. I do what I love to do.

4. I choose to walk in my purpose.

5. I am a magnet for success.

There you go — 30 affirmations to get started. However, much more than giving you a list of affirmations, I also want to empower you to create your own custom-made affirmations and declarations that are specific to you and your objectives.

How to Create Your Own Powerful Affirmations

When it comes to affirmations, there are two major categories: mantra affirmations and goal affirmations (*Dowches-Wheeler, 2021*). While mantra affirmations are usually short and spoken in the present tense as though the said words are already your reality. Goal affirmations are longer and spoken in the present progressive tense as though the actions contained in it are in a state of continual progress.

Here Are Some Examples:

A mantra affirmation is "I effortlessly attract the right client," while a goal affirmation is "I continuously control my own happiness." Although both kinds of affirmations are good, the kind you focus on more are determined by your current belief. For instance, if you want to create affirmations about your business, do you believe you effortlessly attract the right clients? If so, then use more mantra affirmations.

On the other hand, if you are having trouble caring for yourself emotionally, a goal-oriented affirmation helps tilt your beliefs about yourself in the right direction when creating affirmations for well-being. That said, let's go in deeper and look at how to create each kind of affirmation.

Creating Mantra Affirmations

Be the center of your affirmation. Begin your

mantra affirmations with "I." Some people make the mistake of turning the object of their affirmation, such as, "right clients" into the subject of the sentence. But since the goal of this type of affirmation is to strengthen your belief in your abilities, be the focus of your affirmation.

Focus on what you want. Rather than saying, "My decisions are not affected by society's viewpoint of me," say, "I am in total control of my decisions." Avoid the trap of affirming what you do not want. Affirm what you want. Your subconscious mind blurs out the negatives, such as "no," while it processes life through pictures. That's why if I ask you to not think of a big elephant sitting on a tree branch, you immediately form a mental image of what I just asked you not to imagine. This also applies to affirmations. When you use words like "not" in your affirmations, your mind initiates a process that brings up mental images of what you are trying to eliminate from your life. So, basically stay positive!

KISS: **K**eep **i**t **s**tupidly **s**imple! When creating mantra affirmations, your goal should be to make them as concise as possible. This particularly helps you keep it in mind and easily call it back to your conscious memory so that you can repeat it as often as possible. Talking about repeating your mantra affirmations often, try setting reminders on your phone to pop these mantras at different times in your day.

Be present: Instead of using phrases like "I will achieve…", say, "I achieve." Your goal is to train your subconscious mind to tilt toward your affirmations; you don't want it believing that you've not gotten what you seek. Speak as though you have it and watch yourself engage in behaviors that bring your thoughts into manifestation; that's what the concept of a self-fulfilling prophecy means.

Make use of motivating present-tense verbs or adjectives: How does this mantra make you feel? Do you feel loved whenever you are in the company of your friends? Do you feel confident in yourself whenever you successfully complete your tasks? Accompany your mantra affirmations with an adjective that describes how you feel! For instance, instead of saying "I attract the right friends," say, "I joyfully attract the right friends." Rather than saying, "I achieve my career goals," say, "I confidently conquer all my goals." Whenever you attach these positive adjectives to your affirmations, you evoke the feeling associated with that affirmation.

And since mantra affirmations are based on something you believe is true about yourself, your brain remembers this feeling. Then, the brain helps you continually take the actions that will lead to produce more of that feeling. Now, let us touch on another kind of affirmation: goal affirmations.

How to Create Goal Affirmations

Start with the end in mind. As the name implies, you need to know your goals already. And, you don't need to just know these goals. You must also know how it will feel when you've accomplished them. Keep these in mind as you craft your goal affirmations.

Use your superpower words. The words "I am" are the two powerful words. These words commands your subconscious with directives. Be as specific as possible. When creating goal affirmations, you want to describe not just the activity but the feeling the goal evokes in your being. So, rather than using simple, everyday words like "I am buying a car," say "I am happily holding the car keys of my new $75,000 vehicle." Being this descriptive creates a mental picture in your mind, a picture that your brain works to make your reality.

In this chapter, you learned how to write your own positive affirmations and, hopefully, gained an appreciation for their powerful effects. The advantages of developing a growth mindset will be discussed next.

CHAPTER 5: Creating a Growth Mindset

"The mind is just like a muscle – the more you exercise it, the stronger it gets and the more it can expand."

- Idowu Koyenikan

The positive affirmations listed in Chapter 4 are extremely powerful mantras. However, these assertions need fertile soil in which to set roots and transform our lives. The growth mindset described in this chapter is that fertile mental soil.

Oprah Winfrey once said, *"On my own, I will just create. If it works, it works, and if it doesn't, it doesn't. I'll create something else. I don't have limitations on what I think I could do or be."* (*Thoughts on the Business of Life*, n.d.). Oprah's words reflect a growth mindset. This chapter will discuss the difference between fixed and growth mindsets. We will also examine the importance of having a growth mindset and what you need to do to convert your mindset.

Fixed vs Growth Mindset

We cannot escape the need to do new things in today's world. Whether talking to a new person at the party or taking on a new role at work, we must take routes we've never tried before. Unfortunately, we might not succeed on the first try. We make mistakes, and that's typical. However, whether you appreciate not succeeding on the first try as normal will determine your success in life.

In her 2007 book, *Mindset: The New Psychology of Success*, Psychologist Carol Dweck coined the phrases "fixed mindset and growth mindset." A growth mindset views abilities, talents, intelligence, and skills as developing over time and, hence, learnable attributes. Someone with a growth mindset believes she is capable of improving in these areas over time with dedicated effort. On the other hand, someone with a fixed mindset thinks these traits cannot be changed over time. A fixed mindset sees these attributes as inherent rather than developed through consistent practice.

For example, suppose a woman had issues managing a friendship due to bad interpersonal skills. If she has a fixed mindset, she will self-judge that she can never develop good relationships due to her poor interactive abilities. On the other hand, if she approaches this situation with a growth mindset, she will find herself thinking the following. "Well, even though I'm bad at it now, I can read books to develop my interpersonal and communication skills. Even though I lost this friendship, I will use the lessons learned here to improve my other relationships."

While a catastrophic event could serve as a stepping stone for an individual with a growth mindset, the same event could spell disaster for another person with a fixed mindset. This is because those with fixed mindsets believe that if they don't already have the innate skills to carry out a task, there is no possibility of acquiring said skill. So, in a way, having a growth mindset means looking at life through the lens of positivity rather than negativity. This reason is why I want you to want to develop a growth mindset.

Black Women Developing Growth Mindsets

A growth mindset will help you in several ways. First, this type of mindset will enhance your relationships. Also, a growth mindset helps you learn the skills you've always wanted to master.

Moreover, a growth mindset will help you deal with bias in a healthy manner when you encounter it.

A growth mindset can help you live as though biases aren't significant. How? In short, a growth mindset enables you to believe that people are malleable, that people can change over time. And this goes a long way in determining whether you can healthily cope with negative statements and situations. Just so you know, I did not arrive at this conclusion, scientists did.

In collaboration with Carol Dweck, Dr. Rattan conducted research (*London Business School, 2018*) to determine how much outcomes depend on one's belief of whether the person they are dealing with is deliberately hurtful. In summary, the study revealed that those who manage to confront discriminatory remarks feel better than those who fail to face them. The reason for this is quite apparent. When you have a growth mindset, you believe the other person can change. In thinking so, you feel more empowered to confront the bias without attacking the person.

On the other hand, if you have a fixed mindset, you believe that the "basic characteristics" of the individual expressing the bias are unchangeable. Hence, you won't see a need to confront this person's belief system, leading to a missed opportunity to contribute to that person's growth. Hence, the bias persists in that individual, and the situation does not improve. Now, let's see where you stand regarding fixed vs. growth mindsets.

Do You Have a Growth or Fixed Mindset?

Before you attempt the Mindset Quiz, I want to say that if you discover a fixed mindset outcome, don't be too hard on yourself. You were not born with a fixed mindset. If so, how were you able to accomplish walking, talking, or even learning how to ride a bike? As kids, we had growth mindsets. We believed we could do anything regardless of any obstacle we encountered. However, as we grew, we were indoctrinated with the concept of "talent." For example, some of our friends were naturally good at things we struggled at. And in turn, we were good at some things our friends found difficult. With this belief in natural talent, why bother to improve an ability at which you lack natural aptitude? As I said, you were not born with a fixed mindset. Now, I want you to take the Mindset Quiz. These are the rules for the quiz (*Mindset Quiz, n.d.*).

- For each question, circle (or underline) the number that best describes you.
- After completing all 10 questions, total and record your score.
- Use the score chart found after the table to determine the mindset type.

Mindset Quiz

Firmly Agree	Agree	Disagree	Firmly Disagree
A naturally smart person need not to try hard at new things.			
0	1	2	3
I really love learning new things.			
3	2	1	0
My intelligence is a basic characteristic that I can't change.			
0	1	2	3
The more a person engages in a task, the better she gets at it.			
3	2	1	0
I love to get feedback from my family, friends, and colleagues.			
3	2	1	0
Only a few people are good at public speaking. It is an innate ability.			
0	1	2	3
I'm angry when I get negative feedback.			
0	1	2	3
A person can change her intelligence.			
3	2	1	0
Nothing can be done about ones attributes.			
0	1	2	3
You can change how smart you are.			
3	2	1	0

Score:

22 - 30: A stalwart growth mindset.

17 - 21: A solid growth mindset with minor fixed aspects.

11 - 16:   A fixed mindset with capacity for growth ideas.

0 - 10:   A staunchly fixed mindset.

What did you score? If you have a growth mindset, that's great. If you discovered you have a fixed mindset, no worries! The first step to developing a growth mindset is believing you can change it. So, that brings up a question: Do you think you can change your mindset? Well, I do—and so should you! That said, let us check out how you can develop a growth mindset. Cool?

Tips for Fostering a Growth Mindset (*Tryumph, 2021*)

Don't Target Perfection—Instead, Target Progression

When starting anything new, it won't be perfect at first. Let me give an example. Have you ever tried dancing with a move you had in your head? How did that turn out? You probably created a new

78

dance move if you are like me: not a good dancer. This is precisely how going into unchartered waters is. You are very bad at first. But you must never forget that your first try is almost always your worst. Apply this philosophy to new relationships, new career paths, and your first year of parenthood. Your goal should be to make progress every day, even if that means taking only one step forward at a time.

Believe You Can Improve

The battle for whether you will grow or not is won or lost in your mind. If you believe you can, then you can. In other words, you should embrace change.

Refuse to Give Up—Keep Trying

You might not instantly see the progress you want whenever you try anything new, as it may take time. For instance, if your goal is to be physically fit, you won't get your dream body by exercising for only a week. Instead, you must stick to your exercise regimen for an extended period. Remember, just because you can't feel progress doesn't mean you are not making progress.

Redefine Failure

Change how you see failure. Rather than becoming dejected because you didn't hit a goal, see failure as feedback. Focus on the lessons learned from your failure for the next try. This mindset can also be applied when you get personal feedback from people. Realize that you cannot improve when you don't know what to improve. Both failure and personal feedback take the veil off and give you an insight into where you should direct your energy.

Engage the Power of "YET"

When someone asks you if you can do a task, don't give a blunt "no" as an answer. Instead, reply with

something like: "I don't know how to do it YET...."
As short as the three-letter word is, saying YET
often helps you build a platform for your personal
growth. It enables you to convince yourself daily
that you can do anything you want. Remember, the
only limitations are the ones we create in our
minds. Focus on effort, not talent.

When you see people perform effortlessly tasks you
struggle with, there is a temptation to label them as
"talented." While this might be true for some
people, a fire not tended will die out. Hence, at
some point, everyone you see who is talented
nurtures that "talent." The nurturing ignites a fire
that is bright enough for you and others to see it.
"Effort over talent" should be your catch phrase.

Embrace Your Imperfections

Your imperfections show that you are still human.
So, acknowledge them. I don't imply that you
should become content with your limitations, just

that you should not beat yourself up over them. When you view your imperfections negatively, you strip yourself of the chance to work on them.

Take Care in Seeking the Approval of Everyone

In a society that continually views Black women as inferior, it takes a conscious effort not to acquiesce. In cases like this, kindly disprove the idea of inferiority. This is important if you want to develop a growth mindset. Growing means leaving behind old beliefs and philosophies, some shared by people close to you.

Be a Scared Beginner

The journey of a thousand miles begins with a single step, and the master at anything was once a beginner. The first step to getting knowledge is an admission of your ignorance. Be humble about not knowing how to do certain things. Meet with your colleague to have them explain how the process or procedure works. Admit to your partner you need to work on your communication skills. Take courses to sharpen your leadership skills.

Once you have developed a growth mindset, it will feel like you are now in a world of endless possibilities. Limitations disappear, and the barriers you conceived in your mind become non-existent. You then begin to see your personal growth through the lens of positivity. Growth becomes more attainable. However, more is involved for you to develop yourself. Just like in any other important area of life, your personal growth requires that you inject a conscious effort. I will show you how to infuse this conscious effort in the next chapter.

CHAPTER 6: *Prioritizing Personal Growth*

"Personal development is the belief that you are worth the effort, time and energy needed to develop yourself."

- Denis Waitley

As we flex into the growth mindset described in the previous chapter, our personal growth can develop. Still a great deal of the references about personal growth pertains to one's career in the business world. Notwithstanding, these concepts are just as applicable to our personal lives. An exploration of personal growth follows in this chapter.

Of late, there has been a sharp rise in the number of businesses owned by Black women, and that's worth celebrating. However, just like in any other venture, a company's success is judged more by how long it lasts and how well it can scale in the years to come. Therefore, this fact calls for an urgent need to become people capable of leading multi-billion-dollar organizations. The need exists to become women who have consciously learned the principles that allow for a successful business. The process of this "becoming" is known as personal growth.

We all have an area in which we wish to grow. Personal growth doesn't just apply to business. Even if you are not a CEO kind of person, chances are there are things you want to improve in your life. However, given this desire to progress, the question is, where do you begin? That's the question I intend to answer in this chapter.

Does everyone else but you seems to be improving? Does it sometimes seem as though you are in a race? Not a physical, sprint-in-a-track race, but merely one that involves becoming a better person. Do you sometimes feel overwhelmed by how fast everyone else is advancing? People are getting new certifications, becoming better leaders, getting promotions at your workplace, and resolving relationship challenges.

Yet, you are just stuck, not becoming less than who you presently are, but still not yet growing into the ideal "you." So, here's a word of encouragement. That gap between the present "you" and the "you of your dreams" is personal growth.

Personal growth is another word for self-improvement or self-growth (*Sasson, 2016*). We all have weaknesses. These are subpar areas of life coveting improvement. Such weakness may impact your life minimally, such as staying in bed too long and letting the laundry stack up.

On the other hand, weakness may affect your life more dramatically. For example, inefficiency at your job or a lack of understanding of how to maintain close relationships. Either way, even though weaknesses are steadfast in everyone's lives, only we decide how long we want to keep living with them. Then, we can either choose to upgrade that aspect of ourselves or else we can wallow in self-pity. Or, even worse, we can deny the impact of said weakness.

However, since you are reading this book, I'm pretty sure you fall on the first third of the spectrum. You've spotted that you need to work on how to love and care for yourself. Not only did you identify the need, but you also acted by reading or listening to this book. As a result, you are already growing. So, here's another word of encouragement. Even though it might seem you are not making any progress yet—you are. Merely reading this book is a massive step toward self-care. And remember, we appreciate and celebrate all efforts. So give yourself a pat on the back, as you are doing great!

Luckily, that's not even the best part. Involving yourself in activities that lead to your personal growth is akin to building your growth muscle. The impact can extend to other areas of your life. This means, in the same spirit of improving your self-love life, you can go on to enhance any other area of your life. What am I suggesting? You have the power in you. No weakness can habitually keep you down if you decide to make progress. You decide whether you want to stay down or not, by your willingness to act for your own personal growth.

The Brain & Personal Growth

Some decades back, scientists believed that the brain could not grow. They believed that at a certain age, the brain becomes inflexible, and the neural networks become fixed. Fortunately, they've discovered this is not accurate. To understand why this is a massive win for us personal growth enthusiasts, let's go a little into the concept of brain physiology.

Our brains are made up of neurons. These are the structural and functional units of our brain. These neurons have synapses, which are basically intersecting points with other neurons. Neurons connect with other neurons to facilitate communication. Since many neurons work together, the brain's route that carries out activities is called a pathway.

Over time, as we use these neurons, the brain starts to recognize repeated pathways and automates them so that it takes less conscious effort to go through these routes. For instance, do you recall when you began sending messages on your new phone, or the first time you drove to work? Do you remember how difficult it was at first? You had to concentrate on each step. Now, what happened as you carried out these activities repeatedly? It became second nature, right?

This explains the concept of neural pathways (*Boztepe, n.d.*). Just like how it is easier to walk on a path created in the woods, it is simple for your brain to follow an already developed pathway. These pathways direct our routine, everyday habitual activities. From brushing our teeth to automated replies to questions like "How are you?" (We all say "fine," right?).

These neural pathways also make us routinely involved in certain habits, even when we don't necessarily want to behave that way. For instance, have you ever made a New Year's resolution, only to return to your usual way of life by mid-February? Neural pathways make it difficult to give up instilled habits we've developed over the years.

Now, back to the question of whether your brain can change. Like I said, recent studies show that, luckily for us, the brain can change (*Gamma, 2021*). Rather than being rigid, the brain is malleable. This brain flexibility is known as neuroplasticity. With neuroplasticity, new routines can overcome old pathways as we can develop new habits.

So, why is this a massive win for us? Imagine if it was impossible to abandon the old neural pathways associated with bad habits such as a smoking addiction or a tendency to procrastinate. Years went into forming those habits. Of course, it will be challenging to stop indulging in such acts. Since the brain can change, however, this gives us hope that as we consistently attempt new habits, our brain forms newer neural pathways associated with the recent behaviors.

This concept aligns with the law of use and disuse. Anything you use over time gets stronger, and anything not used diminishes. For instance, if a woman stops playing an instrument for months, she will get a little rusty when she returns to the instrument. Likewise, if she plays it consistently every day, she can maintain or improve. Also, when we indulge in better habits and abandon the old ones, we change our outcomes. And this, my friend, is how to accomplish personal growth. But if personal growth is possible, the question is... "What is stopping our personal growth?"

We all know the drill. Being a Black woman in America can be taxing. Denis Waitley stated, *"Personal growth is the belief that you are worth the effort, time and energy needed to develop yourself."* Society would have us believe that we are not worthy. Accepting this attitude begets a reduced rate of personal growth among women of color. Not just that, dealing with this culture's microaggressions results in mental stress accompanied by health challenges, such as depression and low self-esteem. These health conditions impede any effort toward even thinking about personal growth.

Again, some Black women may not see the value in advocating for themselves. Personal growth often involves spending a lot of time working on yourself. You may indulge in such introspective activities as listening to podcasts, and reading books. All these endeavors could be perceived as selfish. Especially when we Black women constantly have others depending on us – such as children, elderly relatives, and friends.

Personal growth may be perceived to come at a cost in terms of time away from doing for our loved ones. Many times, that child needs a meal or help with homework that you, the single mother, are the only person to provide. Of course, our goal should not be to completely abdicate our responsibilities. Instead, we should put in the effort to create the time and resources, so that we can pour back into ourselves. Because, why not? It is high time we take control of our lives. And here's how we can do so.

Your Personal Growth

As the name suggests, personal growth is an intimate pursuit. I've come across myths implying that personal growth should not be considered unless the individual is in the corporate world. This is false. For instance, I know a single mom of two who struggled financially but decided to undertake her own personal growth. So, she took home improvement courses and learned how to decorate a home on a budget. Taking those steps helped her financial life immensely, and she's since doing well.

Please don't misinterpret me. If you are in the corporate world, you can still engage in personal growth. For example, I also know of another Black woman who aspired to reach greater heights in her professional career. She took courses and worked longer hours. Still, even though the process was tedious, her skills and abilities earned her the respect of her colleagues. It also helped her attain her goals. Hence, personal growth is individualized. Thus, I cannot define your personal growth. Just as the saying goes, "Beauty is in the eyes of the beholder." One's definition of personal growth is solely through the lens of the concerned individual.

The ball is in your court. You know your perceived weaknesses are actually disguised opportunities in your life for personal growth. That said, here are five areas of your life you could consider in your bid to find these growth opportunities.

#1 - *Mental Growth*

Mental growth involves increasing your intelligence quotient (IQ) related to specific areas in your life. This includes taking courses and acquiring skills to update your professional knowledge, especially in your field. Merely staying up to date with the latest trends and best practices in your area of expertise is a way to improve your mental aptitude.

#2 - *Social Growth*

Much more than becoming mentally proficient, it's advisable to take time to become socially adept. It goes without saying that we humans are social beings. We thrive in a community and need the power of association to live our best lives. Hence, developing social intelligence through learning effective communication and other interpersonal skills can be extraordinary aspects of your personal growth. In addition, social growth will help you relate with your children better and give you the acumen to improve relationships you deeply care about.

#3 = Emotional Growth

While social growth deals with how you relate with others, emotional development talks about how you connect with yourself and your family. As humans, we deal with feelings. These feelings sometimes can be difficult. When you grow emotionally, you become more proficient at expressing your emotions openly using the right words without initiating conflict. Acquiring this skill greatly reduces the amount of stress and anxiety in your world. Plus, emotional intelligence confers the ability to understand your feelings regarding events surrounding you. It also helps you ascertain the right course of action to change negative emotions and situations without needing to endure them.

#4 = *Physical Growth*

Physical growth involves nurturing and caring for your body, such as eating properly and getting adequate sleep. Furthermore, participating in exercises helps you flourish physically. This is particularly important because the other forms of personal growth hinge on your continued physical health. Unless you maintain good corporal well-being, it's challenging to indulge in other forms of growth. When you do so, you help your brain function better, which translates into an enhanced mind!

#5 - *Spiritual Growth*

Spiritual growth helps you feel part of a larger entity; it gives you purpose and a sense of belonging. When you belong to a community of people who share the same beliefs as you, your stress and anxiety can be greatly reduced.

Personal growth doesn't just come upon you; it requires intentional effort. And I believe these tips will help you navigate the landscape of development.

Understand Your Strengths & Weaknesses

If you don't know where to start, begin here. What are your strengths? What are your weaknesses? Knowing your weakness will give you a perspective for your personal growth, while coming to terms with your competencies serves as encouragement for moments of struggle. Remember your self-love list from Chapter 1? If you are having trouble finding your strengths, bring out your workbook and celebrate the things you admire about yourself.

Expand Your Knowledge

The next tip is to engage in an unemotional search for knowledge. "Unemotional" is the chosen term because sometimes you won't "feel" like going to the gym or reading your book on public speaking. These days, you must choose to "just do it." You might not "feel" the progress, but you are moving, one step at a time! There are several free courses online. Two websites that offer fantastic courses for free are https://www.khanacademy.org and https://www.mooc.org/.

Get a Mentor

Success leaves clues. While you could try figuring it out on your own, getting a mentor will flatten your learning curve. A mentor can direct you to the 20% of activities that yield 80% of the results. You may find a mentor at your workplace. However, if you are not able to find one there, someone with a similar passion for growth can serve as a partner on this journey. In your personal life, mentors are those who have walked the path you wish to take. The generations in front of us have immense experience and knowledge. Just be brave and ask.

Set SMART Goals

Setting goals can motivate you to work when you set out to grow. Plus, setting goals the right way can help you measure how far you've come and the next steps you need to take. SMART is an acronym for *Specific, Measurable, Achievable, Relevant, and Time-Bound*. Try to include all these features in the goals you set. Avoid any vagueness, set key performance indicators (KPIs) alongside your goals (as a way of measuring them), ensure the goals you set are reasonable and relevant to your vision, and attach a time-metric to keep you motivated.

Here's an example. Let's assume today is Sunday, October 1st, and you've just decided to improve your interpersonal skills. So, you go online and find a course that promises to give your communication skills a push. This course is *relevant* to your vision of improving your interpersonal skills. That's great! You then decide to finish the course by the end of the month. Since the course is broken into four sections, you decide to take a weekly unit. This way, by Saturday, you should have finished a segment. This combination makes your goal *specific,* and *time bound.* In addition, the sections are concise, so the goal is *achievable.* Lastly, to make your goal *measurable,* your primary KPI is how you implement what you've learned in your daily activities.

Stay Positive

You might not see immediate results the very day you commit to growing. So, daily doses of positivity can keep you going until the desired accomplishments are realized. Remember those affirmations in Chapter 4? Now is the time to use them in your arsenal against the monster of discouragement!

Before we end this chapter, I'd love to emphasize that personal growth should not just be about developing skills and abilities. Developing a great body image is fundamental for personal growth, which I will deliberate in the next chapter.

If you found this book helpful in improving your life, please leave an honest review on the relevant platform. Reviews are essential for authors - but more than that, your feedback will help other women of color find and benefit from this book too. Thank you in advance for taking the time to share your thoughts!

CHAPTER 7: Body Image & the Black Woman

"Black Girls... Beautiful in EVERY shade and size. We've got that special something! Our melanin is exquisitely beautiful!"

- Stephanie Lahart

In the last chapter, you learned that improving one's talents and abilities are critical aspects of personal growth. In this chapter, I will discuss how important it is to cultivate a positive body image regardless of society's body-shaming messages.

What Is Body Image?

Body image is defined as how a person perceives, thinks, and feels about her body (*Body Image - Women - Better Health Channel, n.d.*). It is the subjective picture or mental image you have of your body. Body image represents a person's thoughts, feelings, and perception of their body's aesthetics or sexual attractiveness. It's not just about shape and weight but appearance in general. There are four aspects of body image (*National Eating Disorder Collaboration, n.d.*).

- *Perceptual* - how you perceive yourself. The way you see your body may not align with your actual appearance.
- *Affective* - the way you feel about your appearance. How satisfied are you with your appearance, shape, weight, and specific body parts?
- *Cognitive* - your thoughts and beliefs about your body. For example, the idea that being thinner will make you feel better and be more attractive.
- *Behavioral* - actions you take because of your perceived body image. People who are unhappy with their appearance may engage in

destructive behaviors like excessive exercise or disordered eating to improve their looks. Some people who are self-conscious about their appearance may isolate themselves.

Body image is how we perceive ourselves physically and the accompanying positive and negative thoughts and feelings, influenced by individual and environmental factors. Consequently, this image can become an excessive focus on comparing your size, shape, or appearance to unrealistic ideals. For example, holding yourself to a thin or athletic ideal may lead to unhealthy self-talk, low self-esteem, or disordered eating patterns.

Ethnic Body Composition Differences

According to researchers, ethnic body composition differences exist (*Gasperino, 1996*). In America, we perceive a notable difference between the body composition of Blacks and non-Blacks. Black women typically have more significant bone and muscle mass but less fat as a percentage of body weight than their White counterparts. Although many Black women might fall into such a category, others don't. Here is why.

Ethnic Groups of Africa

Thousands of different ethnic groups make up Africa. Each of these populations speaks its own language (or a dialect of a language) and practices its own culture (*Wikipedia contributors, 2022a*). There are several major ethnic groups in Africa, such as the Bantu of West and South Africa (*Wikipedia contributors, 2022b*), the Cushite people of the Horn of Africa (*Wikipedia contributors, 2022c*), the tall Nilotic people of Central Africa (*Wikipedia contributors, 2022d*), and the diminutive Pygmies of the Congo Basin of Africa (*Wikipedia contributors, 2022e*). Any cursory study of the varying body types of the ethnic groups of Africa explains the differences in heights, shapes, and leanness reflected in the African diaspora.

We descend from people with a wide range of body types but are constantly media-fed that only one type is the standard of beauty. Just keep in mind that the body type you are gazing at in that media is solely the personal preference of the person with the authority to select that model! Instead, cast your gaze to the Motherland, and you will see your body type reflected in the peoples of Africa.

Healthy Body Image

Positive body image is typically associated with better psychological and physical health. Confidence about your appearance dramatically impacts how you think about yourself and determines your self-esteem. Your self-esteem, in turn, affects every aspect of your life. Higher self-esteem makes it easier for you to manage your day-to-day affairs and be more sociable. These positive intangibles result in elevated levels of satisfaction and well-being. You feel more self-assured and content with how you appear if you have a positive body image. Someone with a favorable body image is less susceptible to being negatively affected by unrealistic media images.

Body Image & Behavior

Your body image is your perception of your body size, weight, shape, and appearance. Your body image is not always directly linked to your actual appearance. Instead, as stated, it is a perception. This perception, however, could be dangerous when it begins to induce behaviors that push your health to the edge. An example of such behavior is dieting or restrictive eating. For example, a woman who views herself as "too fat" might resort to dieting. Sadly, according to the Better Health website, dieting is a strong risk factor for developing an eating disorder.

Again, a negative body image could cause you to develop an unhealthy relationship with physical exercise. For example, you may be that woman who believes she is "too thin," so, you might distance yourself from all forms of physical activity. You might do this because you think exercise will lead to further weight loss. While this may be true, the benefits of physical activity are not limited to weight loss alone.

Exercise significantly impacts the function of our bodies, such as our cardiovascular system and mental faculty. Therefore, physical activity is critical for optimal physical and mental well-being.

Thoughts & Feelings About Your Body

Before you begin your journey toward developing
a more positive body image, let's define positive
body image. The Black woman with a positive
body image feels comfortable in her skin. She
engages in activities that help her develop a good
relationship with her body. A positive self-image
also means redefining beauty — not according to
others' standards, but by your own. Changing
your outward appearance may be challenging and
time-consuming, but altering your perception of
your body is a matter of changing your mind. We
can change how we perceive, experience, and
think about our bodies at any time. So, how do
you become this women with a positive body-
image?

Change Your Perspective

First, it is all about perspective. Focus on what
your body can and has done; the body is amazing.

Appreciating and respecting everything it can do will help you feel more positively about it. Begin with seeing yourself as a whole person rather than an object of intense scrutiny. You are a natural person who is much more than just her physical being. Plus, you are more than a summation of body parts; you are an actual human with a beautiful mind and a fantastic soul. You love effortlessly, and your character is flawless. Think such good things about yourself.

Actively Love Yourself

Be active in your self-love. Focus your attention on the positive aspects of who you are. Tune in to your strengths, abilities, and talents. Doing so can assist you in understanding how to accept and value all you are. Instead, show how much you love yourself by treating your body as a temple. Get a massage. Buy new comfortable clothes. Actively love yourself!

Practice Positive Self-Talk

We've discussed how to create affirmations in previous chapters. And when you come across media messages and pictures that make you feel less than who you are (a Nubian Queen, duh), actively speak out against these messages. You don't know that such messages sow negativity in your heart. So, when you feel such seeds are about to be planted, be quick to remove them from the soil of your mind.

Research has shown that when people criticize themselves, they have more negative feelings, low moods, and negative eating patterns. Instead, make a conscious decision about what you read and visually consume. Remember that most images presented in the media are unrealistic and represent only a small percentage of the population. Remember that they digitally alter those photographs appearing in magazines and online. Thus, as a result, they do not accurately portray the appearance of real people. On the other hand, say positive things to yourself daily; when you say something often enough, you will believe it.

Set Health-Focused Goals

Set positive, health-related focused goals rather than weight loss-related ones. Engage in practices with food and exercise that promote health instead of weight loss. Furthermore, these activities reduce unhealthy eating behaviors by practicing compassion for your body. It is essential to appreciate your beauty and accept your entire being. As a result, you feel more comfortable in your skin. Finally, our goal is to learn to accept our bodies and view ourselves through a lens of love.

Lastly, the great Maya Angelou nodded to the Black woman's body type in her famous poem

"And Still I Rise" (*Poetry Foundation, 1994*) when she wrote:

> *"...Does my sexiness upset you?*
>
> *Does it come as a surprise*
>
> *That I dance like I've got diamonds*
>
> *At the meeting of my thighs?"*

Let us all celebrate that every Black woman's body type is sexy and perfect! We have diamonds at the meeting of our thighs. However, there is a tenuous balance between accepting your body and turning a blind eye to common health risks. Even with a healthy body image, physical health is important. So, this topic is discussed in the next chapter.

CHAPTER 8: Making Health & Fitness Matter

"Your body is precious. It is our vehicle for awakening. Treat it with care."

- Buddha

Kudos for continuing this far on your self-care journey! You are more than half-way there. Summarizing the ideas addressed before this chapter, I presented the concepts of self-love, self-care, the inner child and the adultification bias. Then, I introduced you to such constructs as growth mindset, personal growth, and body image. As established in the previous chapter, every single Black woman's body size is beautiful and ideal in its own way. In this chapter, we will discuss the importance of taking care of our bodies so that we sustain our beauty and health.

Even though our bodies may not fit into the physical stereotypes society has created for us, we remain proud of our physiques. Still, we must recognize when our bodies are subjected to significant health threats. Statistics show that up to 56.9% of Black women in the United States are obese (*Miller, 2022*). And obesity is quite dangerous, given that being overweight is a risk factor for chronic diseases, namely hypertension, diabetes, and arthritis. Thus, we need to pay attention to our weight because, as discussed earlier, physical care is an act of self-love.

Sadly, losing weight is not as easy for us Black women as it is for our fellow White females. A weight loss difference because of race was considered speculation until a study was done to determine the truth of the hypothesis. In the study, 66 White and 69 Black women were placed on the same calorie-restricted diet of 1,800 calories daily for six months. At the end of the time frame, the

Black women lost 8 pounds less, on average than the White women. Chronic stress from racism and discrimination can produce such health outcomes (*Thompson, 2022*).

Hence, it is impossible to follow the same diet plans and exercise regimen as our counterparts and expect the same results. We must create a custom-made weight loss strategy that considers our racial differences. And that's what this chapter will help you do.

Eating Less & Working Out More Is Not for Our Bodies

As Black women, we have a different body composition from non-Black women. Plus, we appear to have a slower body metabolism. So even if we engage in the same routine exercises and workouts, we burn fat more slowly than our White counterparts. In addition, other factors come into play whenever we try achieving our fitness goals. One of them is stress.

After decades of being exposed to systemic racism, it is no surprise to see that Black women live with chronic stress. Much more than that, constant exposure to the combination of race-based and gender-based trauma significantly increases our stress levels. New studies suggest continuous microaggressions may lead to higher stress levels than isolated trauma acts. As a result, when we step out every day into a world that treats us less than we deserve, we respond to the environment in a manner that causes our stress hormone (cortisol) to increase. And when this happens, the heightened cortisol levels in our system serve as a risk factor for obesity, along with other chronic diseases such as hypertension and diabetes.

In addition, "food deserts" often characterize areas of our cities inhabited by people of color. Access to fresh, healthy food is limited for people of color. So, what does this mean for you? First, as you begin your fitness journey, you must assess your life for stressors. Rather than starting with hours of exercise and a weight loss diet plan, stop. Instead, sit down and identify the activities or events that raise your cortisol levels. Then, develop an approach that helps you manage the stress society constantly serves you.

25 Ways to Manage Stress Starting Right Now (*25 Quick Ways to Reduce Stress, 2018*)

The Centers for Disease Control and Prevention (CDC) recommends that people aged 18–60 get at least 7 hours of sleep each night each night to promote optimal health and well-being (*CDC Newsroom, 2016*). However, they found that Black women are getting less than 6 hours, on average (*Johnson, 2016*). Unfortunately, not meeting the required standard of rest exposes us to the risk of obesity and cardiovascular disease. And, what's a better way to purge our cortisol levels than sleep? Not just any type of sleep. By the way, the beneficial effects of sleep are gotten when we enter the "deep zone." In this zone, your liver and pancreas work by clearing away toxins you accumulated during the day.

Most Black women miss the chance to get quality sleep every night, owing mainly to insomnia — the inability to fall or stay asleep. So, before we dive into 25 ways you could manage stress, here are two quick tips that will help your sleep life:

Tip #1 - Invest in Sleep Weapons

You are to spend up to one-third of your life on your bed, so putting some cash aside to upgrade your mattress and pillows might be the best thing you could do for yourself (and your back). If the lights in the neighborhood keep you awake or the sun wakes you up too early, get black-out curtains.

Also, investing in white noise and ear plugs might be helpful if environmental noise keeps you from sleeping.

Tip #2 - Modify Your Nighttime Routine

Are you exposed to blue light before sleep? Research shows that blue light can block melatonin production, which is your sleep hormone. Replace bad bedtime routines such as watching Netflix just before bed with better ones such as meditation and journaling. These mental exercises help relax your nerves and prepare you for a long night's rest.

Now, let's dive into 25 ways you could manage stress in a bid to reduce your cortisol levels:

Get a Stress Ball

There are days the traffic might cause you to miss a presentation or moments you'll wish a punching bag was in sight. A stress ball will come in handy when this happens, as it is a great way to release tension.

Close Your Eyes

We are constantly taking in so much stimulus from the environment. And just like sleep, merely shutting our eyes for as short as 5 minutes can dampen these effects of the environment on us.

Stretch

We sit in chairs for most of the day. Stretching helps relieve the tensions that build up in our muscles. Also, simple posture exercises such as a shoulder roll-out or a chest opening stretch can help you relax after a stressful workday.

Get Away from the Crowd

If you love to be alone, being in a social setting for a long time might create stress and anxiety. When this occurs, take a trip to the bathroom, or simply excuse yourself from the crowd. Spending as little as five minutes away from a crowded environment can relieve stress quickly.

Organize Your Surroundings

No one innately loves a scattered environment. Clutter contributes to the feeling of dismay we sometimes experience. When you suspect that your world is spinning out of control, take a pause and arrange your work desk or your bedroom. It does wonders!

Eat Some Sweets

A few ounces of chocolate help to calm your nerves. I'm not sure if there is research to back this up. But my Nubian Queen, throwing some of that sweet stuff back reminds me that life isn't about thorns, there are some roses in it as well.

Laugh

Try it, just laugh right now! When you laugh, you release the same feel-good hormones released during sex called endorphins. It also decreases stress hormones and increases your body's immunity to diseases. Basically, there are few activities that restore your mind-body balance as fast as a good laugh does.

The "Cold Water" Trick

When the stress hits hard, head to the bathroom and drip some cold water on your wrist. This helps lessen stress as major arteries are just beneath your skin at this location. This practice cools your blood and narrows your arteries to relieve stress.

Music

The trick of giving your spirits a tune-up with good music helps relax your nerves. We all have our favorite songs. So, scream the lyrics at the top of your voice. You will feel empowered to face your stressors. (Caution: Don't do this in public. But still, merely listening to our best songs brings a feeling of peace).

Write it Down

What and how do you feel? Dealing with your thoughts becomes easier when they are clearly defined. Get a pen and paper and pour your emotions on it; be as expressive as possible and watch your stress drop.

Call a Friend

Our mountains look insurmountable until we share them with our friends. You'd be surprised how conquerable your problems are when you talk to a friend about them.

Chew Gum

Any flavor works—simply get a stick of gum into your mouth and chew away your stress.

Sip Green Tea

Green Tea contains L-theanine, a compound that reduces anger levels and diminishes your stress hormones.

Cuddle Your Pet

Pets help us feel accepted, which in turn builds our self-esteem. Snuggle up with your pet if you have had a hard day.

Rub Your Foot on a Golf Ball

Here's a life hack that can come in handy. Buy a golf ball and keep it beneath your work desk. When you feel overwhelmed, take a break, place your foot on the golf ball and roll it back and forth.

Breathe

Slow, deep breathing has been shown to reduce blood pressure. To maximize your breathing, ensure that your exhale last longer than your inhale.

Take a Walk

A quick stroll around the block gives you time to gather your thoughts, and the added advantage of physical activity.

Be Your Own Masseuse

If you need quick relief from stress and don't have a professional masseuse in sight, take matters into your own hands by giving yourself a quick hand massage. Pinpoint the exact point of muscle tension in your body and gently roll your hands over the area.

Find the Sun

The sun has a way of lifting moods. Open your curtains to allow sun rays in. Or better still, go out and have a short romance with the bright guy in the sky.

Count Backward

This sounds a little weird, I know. But, counting from 10 to 1 distracts you from your present thoughts, which are your current source of stress. This doesn't mean you won't deal with these thoughts healthily. However, you can come back to clear the negative thoughts when you are more relaxed.

Try Progressive Relaxation

This involves progressively tensing and releasing different muscle groups in your body, as the name implies. You could begin from the muscles in your toe region and work up to your head and neck.

Fight with the Sweetness of Honey

Do you know that the compounds in honey help improve the oxidative status of your brain while aiding in the fight against depression and anxiety? So, feel free to go ahead and slurp some honey (*Qfrog Labs, 2020*).

Create a Zen Zone

Just like you have a workspace, create a stress-free space. It could be a comfortable chair in the corner of your room or an area in your neighborhood. View this zone as a place where you can go to escape the hustle of daily living.

Do Yoga

There are different yoga styles, but something is consistent. Yoga gives you a good stretch and provides the mental relief you desperately need.

Meditate

Meditation is to your mind what yoga is to your body. Block out time, find a quiet spot, and meditate.

Lifestyle Supporting Black Women's Health

Black women have a 50% higher risk of heart failure compared with White women. Black women are more likely than White women to have a heart attack (*Cleveland Clinic, 2022*). As stated before, the rate of obesity among Black women is alarming. And it is time to do something about it! Nutritionist Maya Feller, who is currently on a mission to reduce these numbers through her foundation, Maya Feller Nutrition, gives us four pieces of advice that will help us do this (*Bondy, 2019*).

Become Educated

Before taking a step toward proper nutrition, you must know your numbers such as your blood pressure, lipid levels, etc. Knowing these and reading up on nutrition-specific approaches will help you understand what food you should run away from and others you should run toward. Again, we must understand the concept of nutrition. Here in America, we are not taught nutrition. Hence, you must take it upon yourself to develop your knowledge of nutrition and how it affects you.

Don't Dismiss, Substitute

The problem with your current diet might not be the food itself and could be the manner of preparation and the additives. Little changes go a long way! For instance, air-frying your plantain instead of oil frying it and replacing white bread with whole grain bread will help you to consume a better diet.

Get Creative with Physical Activity

When we think of "physical activity," we often imagine a woman with sweat dripping down her face and wind rushing against her body. While that can be true, physical activity could also mean taking a 10-minute walk. So, even though you might not have the liberty to dedicate a specific time for exercise, getting off the subway or the bus one stop before yours or taking the stairs rather than the elevator would count as physical activity. You could also get creative by turning your everyday, mundane tasks, such as vacuuming, into aerobic exercise by integrating dancing and body stretches into them.

Educate Those in Your Circle

You oversee getting the groceries in your home. So, educate others in the house. Explain how important it is to consume natural foods over processed meals.

Exercise Your Body & Mind

Before we go into the details about exercise, let's talk about the mindset you must have before you begin your healthier body journey. Begin small. For example, imagine there are two women embarking on the same health journey: "Woman A" and "Woman B". Both women are obese and determined to shed some pounds. So, "Woman A" goes all in with a strict diet and a draining exercise regimen. However, "Woman B" starts with baby steps. She makes tiny changes in her lifestyle, such as taking daily 5 minutes walks and stretching.

Although she adjusts her diet, "Woman B" ensures she has treats for her efforts and that she is not too hard on herself.

After 2 weeks, which of these women do you think will still be going strong? The answer is a no-brainer - Woman B! You see, the healthier body journey requires consistency. That's why we cannot eat the entire elephant in one bite! Pursue your health goals one bite at a time. Simplicity promotes consistency; start simple and increase intensity each week. That's what leads to results!

Having said that, let's look at "*9 Badass Black Women*" who are changing the exercise game.

9 Badass Black Women Changing the Exercise Game (*Holland, 2021*)

1. *Brittne Babe*

   Website: Brittnebabe.com

   On her YouTube channel, she helps people become fitter by taking them through a series of full-body exercises broken down into different target areas (*Holland, 2021*).

2. *Keaira Lashae*

   Website: teamlashae.com, YouTube: Move Fitness

   Have you ever tried a dance workout? I bet not! Keaira, on her YouTube channel, is changing how we view and engage in exercise. It doesn't have to be difficult. It could also be you moving to your favorite song.

3. *The BKBooty Fitness*

   YouTube: The BKBooty Fitness

The BKBooty Fitness helps you strengthen your core, butt, thighs, and calves by offering high intensity Pilates and cardio workouts.

4. *Kola Olaosebikan*

   YouTube: Koboko Fitness

   Although she lacks a website, her YouTube channel is enough to give us access to all the sauce she offers. She provides lots of High-Intensity Interval Training (HIIT) workouts. Plus, none of her exercises involves equipment, which is excellent (*Holland, 2021*)!

5. *Jessamyn Stanley*

   YouTube: Jessamyn Stanley

   As a positive body advocate and yoga instructor, Stanley takes us deep into the world of yoga with her expertise in vinyasa flow. This is particularly good because it serves as a form of physical activity and is also excellent for your mental health.

6. *Toni Mitchell*

   YouTube: Toni Mitchell

   She's also into the HIIT workout niche, but rather than just sticking to a YouTube channel, she also has a dedicated Instagram account where she offers workout reels. Her "9 Minute Fat Burning Morning Routine" might be precisely what you need to start your day, quickly and efficiently!

7. *Selena Watkins*

   Instagram: Selenawatkins

   Do you want to feel like you are celebrating and not working out? Selena's Socanomics dance gets you in the groove — even if you are rhythmically challenged.

8. *Abiola Akanni*

   Instagram: yogaabybiola

   As an all-encompassing self-care routine, Abiola Akanni offers yoga programs that help align the physical and mental. They offer stretches, help you to release your tensed muscles, and provide relief from nagging thoughts.

9. *Kanoa Greene*

Instagram: Kanoagreene

One look at her Instagram page, and a bolt of positivity will come at you. Her workouts are created for real people living real lives. The excitement and enthusiasm she brings to the table are enough to send anxiety and intimidation out the window (*Holland, 2021*).

Our exquisite bodies require care to maintain health. Caring for one's physical body can be a solitary or group activity. As human beings, we women all need relationships and support systems. Every Black woman needs a tribe of supporters. The next chapter examines the importance of relationships and how to build the support systems we all need.

CHAPTER 9: *Relationships & Support Systems*

"Behind every successful woman is a tribe of other women who have her back."

- Anonymous

In chapter 8, we showed that the movements involved in taking care of one's physical body can be done alone or in a group setting. Still, however way you choose to move, every Black woman needs her own group of supporters. We need each other to get through times of loss, trouble, or trauma, as well as to celebrate and rejoice. We are compelled to support, honor, and make room for our autonomy, fight for our lives, and remind each other of our value and that none of us is disposable. We must remember, talk about, and use strategies for being rooted, getting support, and becoming resilient. Let's return to meeting these requirements as a community.

In this chapter, I will discuss the importance of relationships for a Black woman's self-care. I then end with a look at healthy boundaries. Relationships with oneself, supportive relationships, and healthy boundaries all play a part in keeping you feeling loved and worthy.

Relationships with Others - Building a Support System

Once you curate self-knowledge, it's easier to build other relationships that reflect the qualities you value. Healthy connections with others are key to achieving optimal self-care. So, the second-most important relationships are the ones you have with those who love and support you. In a world that tells you to be an island, it's easy to feel like caring for yourself is selfish and indulgent. But please believe that, on the contrary, your relationships with others are important assets in your self-care toolbox. So, seek out people who support your journey toward self-care. These people can be friends, family members or even a counselor. When we surround ourselves with positive people who believe in us and want us to succeed, it makes reaching our goals that much easier!

What if we replace that term "strong" with "supported" in describing Black women? We all instinctively know the importance of relationships. Having a community of friends who support you through your highs, lows, ups, and downs is a gift that cannot be quantified. Self-care is not just about taking care of yourself only. It's about caring for oneself in a way that allows you to help others, too. And when we say "others," we don't just mean your friends and family — we're talking about the people in your community like those who live near you, work, study, or worship with you. Everyone deserves the chance to be cared for, and everyone benefits from being part of a community that takes care of each other.

Relationships are vital for Black women because they provide support, insight, and validation, as is true for all humans. These connections help us feel less alone, which is important for self-care. If there are people in your life who are ready to help you heal, and grow, take advantage of their presence! They make a difference because they are members of your tribe or your royal court. Really, if you don't have any people in your life who can support you — emotionally or physically — then what kind of self-care are you practicing?

Black women are often told to "be their own best friend." This is a good start, but it's not enough. To truly take care of yourself, you need to build relationships that support and encourage you. You might be thinking: "But I don't have those types of friends who support my goals and dreams." If this is the case, it's time to make new friends who will help you get where you want to go. If you do not currently have anyone in your life who can support you through this process, then finding someone in real life or online may be helpful! Here are a couple tips for making those new relationships happen:

- Make a list of people in your life who inspire you or make you feel safe, and then reach out to them! You can ask them for help with something specific — like a recommendation for a therapist — or just say "hi" and let them know how much they mean to you.

- If no one comes immediately to mind when thinking about who might be able to help you out with self-care, try joining an online community where people share similar interests or experiences as yourself. You can find these communities on social media platforms like Facebook or Instagram. Look for groups that relate to your interests or hobbies (for example, self-care for Black women). For those of us who are not into social media, a list of 41 organizations or communities that support Black women is at the end of this chapter.

Still, not everyone can pick up the phone or hop on an electronic device and get involved with the above listed organizations so easily. How about just cultivating some relationships with neighbors or with the people you find yourselves running into all the time--that nice mom who always is at the daycare when you pick up your child, or that older lady who lives alone upstairs. Often friendship starts with sensing who is like us or apt to be supportive of us among the strangers we meet.

Please remember that for healthy boundaries to be established, a healthy relationship with oneself is critical. Without this, it is impossible to know what is best for you, or even if you want something different than what you're currently experiencing.

When we develop understanding relationships with other people in our lives, we are better able to maintain healthy boundaries. Such relationships also provide a structure for connecting with the world around us and offering support when we need it most. Finally, there needs to be an awareness of healthy boundaries so that we can protect ourselves from people who may seek out our weaknesses to use them against us later.

Healthy Boundaries

Once we reach out to the world and connect to helpful people, we must establish and maintain healthy boundaries so that we can balance our own needs and those of other's. Beneficial limits are needed to keep others from interfering with your path toward self-care. Boundaries protect our personal or mental space, much like fences between neighbors. They involve the physical and emotional limits of appropriate behavior between people and help define where one person ends and the other begins.

There are many different types of boundaries (*Brooten-Brooks. 2022*) including:

- *Emotional:* Relates to feelings and personal details. These boundaries are crossed when feelings or personal information you have disclosed is belittled, minimized, or shared without your permission.

- *Financial:* Involves your financial resources. This boundary is crossed when you're pressured to spend or loan money when you would prefer not to.

- *Mental:* Includes your personal ideas, beliefs, and thoughts. A healthy boundary respects that others' ideas may be different. These boundaries are crossed when someone dismisses, belittles, or invalidates your ideas or thoughts.

- *Material:* Affects your possessions. This boundary is crossed when you're pressured to lend or give belongings away.
- *Physical:* Incorporates your body and personal space. Healthy boundaries include autonomy of your body. An example of physical boundary crossing is requiring children to always hug all relatives at family gatherings. Offering a handshake or just a "hello" are polite alternatives.
- *Sexual:* Concerns your sexual and your intimate personal space. Sexual boundaries include choices around types of sexual activity, timing, and partners. These boundaries are crossed when someone pressures you into unwanted intimate affection, touch, or sexual activity.
- *Time:* Pertains to how you spend and use your time. When you have a job, relationships, and children or other responsibilities, it's challenging to keep healthy time boundaries. These

boundaries are crossed when you have unreasonable demands or requests of your time, or when you take on too much.

Healthy boundaries help us protect ourselves from people who may not have our best interests at heart, or who may be taking advantage of us in some way. Relationships with others can be challenging at times, but it is important to remember that there are healthy boundaries in place. Healthy relationships allow us to interact with others while still being true to ourselves and our values, which plays an important role in self-care. There's no such thing as perfect self-care. And there's no shame in admitting that sometimes we all need help from others to get ourselves back on track. In fact, admitting this is an incredible act of strength—because it means that you know yourself well enough to be honest about where your limits lie.

But what about those relationships that don't support our growth? It's simple: we draw boundaries! Boundaries are a way of saying "this is what I need from this relationship" and "this is how much I'm willing to give." You can set boundaries for yourself as well as for others—and you should! It's your life, after all.

When it comes to relationships, it's important to remember that everyone has different needs and desires. That's why it's so important to develop boundaries and respect others' as well. Setting and communicating personal limits are crucial for our safety, health, and wellbeing, even though it can be difficult to do so. The term "border" can be somewhat deceptive. It expresses the notion of maintaining your own space. But since limits offer wholesome guidelines for managing relationships, whether intimate or professional, they are intersections for connection.

We can establish boundaries for: personal space, sexuality, emotions, thoughts, belongings, time, and energy; as well as things like culture, religion, and ethics. Healthy boundaries have advantages for those in the relationship such as improved self-worth, increased independence and agency, and emotional energy conservation. Setting boundaries enables you to put your needs first, whether they relate to relationships, job objectives, or self-care.

Setting Healthy Boundaries

"It is important to know your basic human rights when setting boundaries," says Judith Belmont, a licensed psychotherapist and author who writes about mental health (*Chesak, 2018*). Once these rights are respected, you won't have to try to appease others. Here are some examples of what she means (*Chesak, 2018*).

Important Rights

- To say "no" without feeling guilty.

- To be treated with respect.

- To regard my needs as equally important as those of others.

- To accept my mistakes and failures.

- To refuse other people's unreasonable expectations of me.

Boundary Setting

- Be confident. Use "I" statements.

- Learn to say "no." "No" is a complete sentence.

- Protect your personal space and schedule "non-negotiable" time alone.

Recognizing Your Self-Worth

You will have heard of self-worth at some point. Perhaps, you have even read a book on it. But, after getting so much information, why do we sometimes find ourselves stumbling? I will tell you why. We are emotional beings rather than rational beings.

Today, I implore you to reassess your self-worth, as an esteemed Nubian Queen. As you do this, understand the direct correlation between your self-worth and the success of your relationships. For example, how much do you value the things you love above what the world says you should love? How much importance do you place on your own values?

Equally important to keeping healthy boundaries is knowing when to reach out to others, especially supporting other Black women, which would likely also lead to friendship. We don't all have to be islands. Islands are over-rated. We all need each other.

Your self-worth is the bucket that holds the water of love people pour into you. This self-worth bucket will have holes if you maintain low self-esteem. As a result, you will not be able to receive the love and support others give you. For example, your partner could love you so much. Yet, you won't be able to feel this love if you don't value yourself. But, on the other hand, a great sense of self bolsters you to feel every drop of love others shower on you — because you are worth it, my Nubian Queen!

Finding Outside Support

Isolation could be a massive punch in the gut, especially if you don't have a partner or intimate friends. However, if you are looking for a community of people who truly understand what it means to be a Black woman, here are 41 organizations or spaces that support Black women. In these communities, you will find like-minded women who can relate to your circumstances. From there on, friendships will sprout, and relationships will blossom.

41 *Organizations or Spaces That Support Black Women* (*Cuzzone, 2021*) & (*Candelario, 2021*)

1. Black Girls Code
2. The Audre Lorde Project
3. Black Emotional and Mental Health
4. Black Girl In Om
5. Black Girls Smile Inc
6. Black Mamas Matter Alliance
7. Black Women's Blueprint
8. Black Women's Health Imperative
9. Black Youth Project 100
10. Buy from a Black Woman
11. Dive in Well
12. DRK Beauty
13. Essie Justice Group
14. Ethel Club

33. The Boris Lawrence Henson Foundation

34. The Foundation for Black Women's Wellness

35. The Loveland Foundation

36. The National Black Women's Justice Institute

37. The Okra Project

38. The Secret Lives of Black Women

39. Therapy for Black Girls

40. Ujima Community

41. Viva Wellness

Above, we discussed the relationship with oneself and others. Now, let's talk about one of the most formidable relationships in existence — the connection between a mother and her child. In this type of bond, we can be sure to cultivate values in our kids. Such values include self-love and an unbending confidence in their abilities, skills, and prowess, as well as spirituality. In the next chapter, we will go deeply into the mother-child relationship, which is one of life's most fulfilling human experiences.

CHAPTER 10: Children - It Takes a Village

"Love felt by the parent does not automatically translate into love experienced by the child."

- Dr. Gabor Maté

The previous chapter discussed intimate and supportive adult relationships for Black women. However, the mother-child rapport is one of the most significant and influential connections in the world. This critical relationship provides us women of color the opportunity to instill appropriate values in our children and affect future generations. These values include self-love as well as unwavering confidence. In this chapter, we explore even deeper this essential relationship between Black women and our children.

Being a mother has never been more challenging. As moms, we protect our kids, but protection requires much more than goodwill. Let me give an instance. Do you remember the Uvalde Elementary School shootings? I looked at those parents with tears trickling down their faces. They wondered if they would hug or bury their child that day. I couldn't help but become more anxious about my own kid's safety. What's more, when my child arrived home the same day, he heard the news. Out of his cute, innocent mind came questions like "Why did he shoot those kids?" Also, "Did the kids make him mad?" I got even more alarmed.

How can I comfort my child? How was I going to convince him that he was safe when I had not even convinced myself? Statistics show that Black people are 12 times more likely to be killed by a gun than White people. This statistic is terrifying! The job of protecting our children requires much more grit and skills than it did a few decades back. In this chapter, I will show you a few tips that have worked well for me and others. You can implement these tricks immediately to increase your faith in your parenting ability.

Loving the Color of Their Skin

Let's not shy away from the truth. We are in a society that is constantly at war with people of color. Even when we are not confronted face-to-face, acts of racism have been knitted deep within the fibers of our social, cultural, and legal systems. But that's a discussion for another day. Racism is an evil of society. So, we gradually try to address the underlying issues. In the meantime, we must equip our children with enough weapons to defend their mental well-being against the daily onslaught they face. The first of such weapons is an understanding of their uniqueness: the color of their skin.

As mothers, one of the critical components of our job is teaching our kids to love the color of their skin. When they go to school, other kids will express ideas that might cause our children to doubt the uniqueness of their color. Still, with persistence, we can imbue them with how beautiful they are because of their skin color. Teach your kids to love their color in several ways. First, compliment your children often. Tell your kid that she is not beautiful just because of her dazzling clothes. Instead, tell her she is beautiful just because of who she is. Black is beautiful! Let her know.

Secondly, immerse your youngster in diversity. It may seem daunting to your kid to love her skin color when she is surrounded by many opposing messages. However, exposing your child to the world's diversity of cultures teaches her to relate to people beyond the superficiality of their skin color.

As an alternative, what you want her to use to determine the value of other humans in her world based on their heart's intent. And when this happens, your cute little one will not only see others how you've taught her to but will also see herself that way. She will notice that the "heart's intent is *good*," so their skin color doesn't matter. This will make her begin to love herself more as a child — long before societal voices strive to change her viewpoint about space in the world.

So, grab your car keys, head for the door, and bolt to diverse cultural settings. It could be a Chinese restaurant, an African museum, an Indian establishment — any environment that helps expose your child to diversity. Not just excursions. Reading also helps. Read a lot of diverse books that are all-inclusive and celebrate diversity.

Arm Our Children Against Racism

While teaching your child to value his skin color, it is problematic to place a focus on the high prevalence of racism in our society. This will be counterproductive, as whatever you focus on magnifies in our child's world. Furthermore, emphasizing racism causes your kid to become more conscious that some people don't value his skin color. Thus, there is a risk of this ideology encroaching on his mindset. Hence, the focus of your discussion should not be racism (*Davenport, 2022*).

However, this doesn't throw the problem out the window. You want your kid to be more solution-aware than problem-focused. Your aim should be to arm your child against the menace of racism. For instance, educational institutions focus more on historical White figures and often neglect Black history. A wrong way to approach this form of systemic racism would be to blame and talk trash about the system with your kid, because this approach will only make him more problem-aware. On the flip side, a better way to approach this is to educate your child on his rich culture. Now, that's being solution-focused.

The Talk

Dr. Riana Anderson and Dr. Shawn C.T. Jones researched Black families over the past 40 years (*Moving "The Talk" to "The Walk" for Black Children, 2021*). They identified four common strategies Black families use when having racial conversations with their children. While all approaches produce outcomes, the results from the last two methods aren't sustainable. So, I would advise you to focus on the first two strategies.

The first approach is cultural socialization or pride. In this case, the family showcases their rich Black history and teaches the children to value their cultural background. This also involves learning songs, reading books, watching movies, and generally engaging in activities that promote their rich Black heritage.

The second strategy is a concept known as "preparation for bias." This approach is offered to kids to prepare them for imminent racial sentiments. For instance, teaching your kids what to do and where to put their hands when pulled over by a police officer is a form of preparation for bias.

Now, to the third. This is called the "promotion of distrust or mistrust." Suppose you had bad racial experiences while growing up. In that case, it could be tempting to label the group of people who took you through such an ordeal and then tell your children to stay away from "them." In this way, you build a wall between the children and this group of people with distrust. We are all humans, and it is common to train our kids out of the abundance of our own experiences. However, this strategy often leads to anxious and depressed kids, as it may be difficult for our youths to cope due to the weight of distrust placed on them.

Lastly, the fourth strategy is known as egalitarianism. This means turning an entirely blind eye to the racial situation of society. Then again, rather than not talking about it, this strategy involves actively telling our children that "everything is good" when it is obviously not. The approach might work at first. But, in the long run, when kids come face-to-face with the realities of society, it may become too psychologically challenging for them to deal with the truth once hidden from them.

Teach Empathy (*Dewar* 2022)

Research shows that being empathetic is an excellent way of helping those who experience racism. However, if you believe that empathy is an innate talent or a gift that people have more or less of, you might find this strange. This is far from the truth. Empathy can be learned. Developing compassion depends on the child's environment and whether they are exposed to quality social interactions, meeting their needs or communication style.

The benefits of empathy are enormous, primarily when used as a coping skill in the face of racism. For instance, if your compassionate child is picked on by another at school because of his skin color, empathy will help him understand that it might not necessarily be the other child's fault. People are not born racist; it is learned from the environment, especially close relatives. Empathy allows our children to look at the world from another individual's perspective. And this skill will prove helpful in years to come.

In a bit, I will show you how to teach empathy to your offspring. But before that, I should affirm that empathy isn't forgiveness. Or rather, compassion doesn't mean simply overlooking people's faults without correcting them. Instead, consideration simply helps an individual step into another's shoes. And while in those shoes, one realizes that the person may not have begun life as a racist. So then, it is possible to not end up as one later in life, even if the influence of society or their own upbringing has made them so right now. That said, let's talk about practical ways of teaching this crucial skill to your little one.

First, give children the support they need to develop self-regulation skills. Empathy involves feeling, most times, the negative emotions of others. Unless we train our kids to understand and manage their own negative emotions, they will shrink away from it in others. Hence, emotional coaching should be one of your top parental priorities. Earlier in this book, I showed you how to deal with negative emotions healthily. So, let's take this knowledge and impress it into our children.

Play Empathy Games Daily

For example, imagine a kid who didn't bring lunch to school on a particular day. He is hungry, but no one lends him a hand because he is considered a nerd. Fortunately, you have enough in your lunchbox to share that day. "What will you do?" Ask your child this question. But just before he answers, ask him to pause and reflect on how this hypothetical boy may be feeling. Do this every day and watch your child's empathic muscles bulk up.

Help Your Child Discover Commonalities

Research shows that when people discover that they are like each other, they find it easier to show empathy toward each other. So, integrate the concept of similarity into your empathy game. For example, ask your child to think of ways he is like his sister, father, or even the kid at school. When he is asked this consistently, he will begin to perform these gracious acts unconsciously.

Have Open Discussions About Race

This brings us back to what I shared in the session about "The Talk." I encourage you to avoid taking a "color-blind" approach to discussing race. Instead, talk about it openly. If you don't, pop culture will! Help your child perceive the world through the eyes of people from other races, as this perception will promote empathy.

Gentle Parenting

Parenting doesn't come with a manual, and one of the things that we exhibit unconsciously is the parenting style from our childhood. For example, decades ago, corporal punishment was a standard within the Black community. And although this was done with goodwill at heart to keep children safe, beatings led to generational trauma. So, now it is your turn to take up the baton. Please stop this kind of trauma in your lineage. Also, take up a more child-centered approach in your parenting. Here's where gentle parenting comes in.

Gentle parenting takes the "the only way you get someone to do something is by making them want to do it" approach. It is a form of parenting that involves a partnership between the child and the parent, leading to the child making decisions born out of an internal willingness rather than external pressure. Traditional parenting often deals with punishment and reward. On the contrary, gentle parenting establishes healthy boundaries and focuses on understanding the child's behavior instead of immediately administering punishment.

When parents hear of this style, they think of it as boundary-free. As a mom, it can be scary to imagine losing your hold over your kid, and it is easier to use punishment. Conversely, gentle parenting involves self-discipline on the part of the parent. However, this gentle parenting style is not from anger that your kid didn't obey "your" rules. On the contrary, this discipline is presented in the form of messages from a "child-centered" approach.

For instance, your kid throws a tantrum because you don't want to buy her another chocolate bar at the store. The traditional approach would involve yelling phrases like, "You've had enough chocolates today. Stop acting childish, put your shoes back on and let's go home! If you don't, I will discipline you at home." Now, because your kid identifies you as an authority figure, this behavior will temporarily cease. But unfortunately, this event is bound to repeat itself.

Instead, you can approach the same situation with a gentle parenting style. You stoop to eye-level with your child and say, "I understand that you want another chocolate bar. But you had enough already today. Taking another one might not be good for your body. We are running late already; if you don't stop crying, you may lose certain privileges."

You will notice both styles involve communicating some sort of discipline. However, gentle parenting involved an extra bit of humanity. This is because this parenting style lies in the three fundamental principles of empathy, understanding, and respect. That said, let's begin with empathy.

Empathy

We don't get breaks in this parenting job. And it is tempting to turn on auto-pilot mode. However, empathy is a reminder to slow down and feel what your child is feeling. Doing this will help you stop lashing out from a place of anger and start reasoning with your child based on the compassion you experience.

Understanding

Kids are kids. Do we even realize this? So often, we treat kids as adults. We rationalize their obviously childish requests with an adult mind. Why would they want to stay back at the park when their playtime is over? Why would they throw tantrums at the school gate? We see all these scenarios through the lens of an adult mind. The problem is not the action; it is the lens through which we see it. Understanding, involves remembering to consider our juveniles as children, who emotionally are not

174

as developed as we grown-ups are. Therefore, it is unwise to treat them as adults.

Respect

Quit seeing yourself as an authority figure and begin viewing yourself as a supporter. A champion won't issue harsh orders as though they are a military commander. Instead, a collaborator makes requests. Respect means honoring your children and asking their consent (when appropriate) before making decisions that affect them. If you are confused about how to integrate gentle parenting into your everyday life, here are some tips;

- Separate the actions from the person. Kids are humans, and all humans make mistakes. Instead of saying, "You made your sister mad," say, "How you behaved caused your sister to get angry." Minor changes like this help you to recognize that certain habits don't define your kid.

- Instead of demanding, invite. This stems from respecting your child as a human. Don't say, "Brush your teeth." Instead, say, "Should we brush your teeth now?"
- Model kindness. This means being kind to not only others but also yourself. And verbalize this act of kindness so your child can hear you say it and see you do it. Side note — this is an excellent way of teaching your kid empathy too!

Leading by Example

Much more than hearing, kids learn by observing. So, the best way to train your kid to love himself might be to love yourself. Be very loud about it. For example, when you are tired, tell him, "I am exhausted today. I think I will need to take a cold shower and then go to bed early tonight." Or when you feel stressed, say, "I will be taking the day off work today to rest my head. Mom feels stressed a little." Doing this will give your child a heads up on how to treat herself in a similar situation.

In this chapter, we explored the crucial connection between Black moms and our children. Aside from taking care physically and emotionally of yourself and your offspring, your spirituality also plays a part in teaching them how to lead a happy and fulfilled life. As you will see in the next chapter, these benefits are enormous.

Another book by this author, entitled "Positive Affirmations for the Black Child - Self Talk for the Child of Color," contains affirmations that are geared toward enhancing the self-esteem of children of color. I hope these affirmation become the foundation of your child's self-talk.

CHAPTER 11: *Embracing Spirituality*

"The spiritual journey is the unlearning of fear and the acceptance of love."

– Marianne Williamson

The importance of Black mothers to their children was discussed in Chapter 10. But in addition to how you relate to your child, your faith also plays a role in teaching your child how to lead a happy life. These advantages are tremendous. But before you can teach it to your child, you have to forge your own spiritual path. This chapter addresses the spirituality for the self-caring Nubian Queen.

An estimated 4,200 religions, faiths, cultures, and movements exist, each promoting its own beliefs and ethics. Therefore, it is impossible to find common ground among so many differing belief systems. However, the one commonality — regardless of our tribe or sentiments — is that we are all spiritual beings. And if so, we all have the innate ability to live a more spiritual life and reap the abundant benefits that spirituality guarantees. Pierre Teilhard de Chardin says, "We are not human beings having a spiritual experience. We are spiritual beings having a human experience." When we embrace this truth, our spiritual world expands and bestows us with an enriching existence during our brief time in this world.

In this chapter, we will focus on integrating certain "*modest*" spiritual acts into your daily living as self-care practices. But before we go into detail about the spiritual activities you could get involved in, let's start with the basics.

What Does It Mean to Be Spiritual?

To begin, let's be clear that spirituality isn't religion. Although both share some similarities, there are notable differences as well. The concept of spirituality stems from our ever-continuous search for purpose and meaning as human beings. Since we've all pondered this question at some point, we can conclude that spirituality is not an isolated experience, not meant for only a select group of people. Instead, it is a universal human experience. While some people find their sense of spirituality in a religion or faith, others find it by becoming connected with nature or artistic expression.

As I previously stated, religion and spirituality have similarities. Nevertheless, they also have notable differences. Religion refers to an organized set of beliefs subscribed to by a group of individuals. On the other hand, spirituality is defined by the individual – herself. And the meaning of the spiritual practice is imbued by said individual. Therefore, while a religious person can be spiritual, being spiritual doesn't necessarily confer on you a religion. Still, the benefits of faith cannot be underestimated.

However, regardless of how we manifest our spirituality, the nurtured connection between our inner (true) self and something bigger than us promotes peace, gratitude, and acceptance. Once we enjoy peace, gratitude, and acceptance, these become gifts we can dole out to those in our orbits (*What Is Spirituality?, n.d.*).

Earlier, I mentioned that there's a difference between spirituality and religion. While spirituality may incorporate some aspects of a religion, religion remains a subset of spirituality. That said, let's bring this back home. How does spirituality relate to self-care? Perhaps, the best place to understand that is to see how spirituality affects our health.

Health Benefits of Spirituality

The advantages of spirituality with respect to our health are numerous. However, let's focus on just four of them.

Improved Emotional State

Usually, spirituality involves engaging in activities alongside people who share the same beliefs as you do. With this spiritual community in place, you can easily ward off any feeling of isolation associated with specific emotional troubles. Plus, a spiritual group opens you up to a broader support system— people who share your perspective and understand what you are going through.

Stronger Immune System

Many aspects of our lives can create concerns and stress. For example, workplace racism and sexism and feelings of inadequacy are voiced regularly as stress factors. Unfortunately, stress can adversely affect your immune system. Finding your spirituality encourages practices that help your body relieve stress, strengthens your immune system, and improves your health (*Sagelife Senior Living, 2021*).

Lower Risk of Disease

Stress is not only detrimental to your immune system, but is also a risk factor for several chronic and acute diseases. One such example is hypertension. The positive feelings accompanying spirituality can relieve stress and invariably lower your risk for some health conditions.

Longevity

According to research carried out by Mayo Clinic, people who are spiritual live longer (*Sagelife Senior Living, 2021*)! Better confidence and fitness are by-products of practicing spirituality. Some people choose activities such as yoga, outdoor walking, and exercising as their spiritually physical outlets.

These individuals become more fit and enjoy a better sense of well-being as well as such benefits as lower blood pressure. Likewise, they become more confident. However, even if you don't engage in physical activities as you embrace spirituality, feeling welcomed by your spiritual community boosts your sense of well-being. Now that you understand the impacts spirituality can have on your health, it's time we dive into some spiritual activities in which you can engage.

Mindfulness & Meditation

Mindfulness

The most basic definition of mindfulness is act of paying attention to the things that you are experiencing. Have you ever heard the phrase, *"be fully present, aware of where we are and what we're doing,"*? It's an attempt to draw us into a world where we are focused on the here and now. Meditation is the essential human ability to be aware of who we are, where we are, and what we are doing now. It enhances our ability to be in the present (*Brown, 2021*). While this might seem like something trivial, it is not easy to accomplish. For instance, how often have you sat to work at your desk to find yourself completely lost in a world of self-draining thoughts 20 minutes later?

Our minds easily wander. Mindfulness is being able to bring the mind back to focus. The practice of mindfulness helps us slow down and be present, rather than focusing on the past or being anxious about the future. If this concept is new to you, getting the hang of it can be challenging.

Meditation

Meditation is an ancient practice that helps people go deeper within themselves so that they can experience a more profound and connected sense of their true self and their realities. Meditation has been practiced for thousands of years. It continues to be a respected practice by spiritual leaders, traditions, and religions. The main goal of meditation is to make you feel spiritually connected, mentally clear, emotionally calm, and physically relaxed at the same time.

Difference Between Mindfulness & Meditation

Meditation is by its very nature mindful, but it could be said that it takes us beyond our minds and helps us grow in ways that basic mindfulness doesn't. Some people might say that mindfulness is a type of meditation, but practicing mindfulness doesn't have to be meditative all the time. Even if you are fully present in this moment, you might not be able to reach a meditative state or go beyond the mind.

It's possible that mindfulness brings us so firmly into the present moment that we become aware of the things our minds do and how they act. Meditation, on the other hand, helps us rise above, go beyond, or replace our thoughts. Nonetheless, for the purpose of this discussion the term mindfulness meditation will be used to discuss these activities.

Mindfulness Meditation

Mindfulness meditation is one of the simplest ways to meditate. The main idea is that you should choose to calmly pay attention to your actions, feelings, and thoughts as they happen, without thinking about the past or the future and without any assumptions, conditions, or judgments.

When you walk through a park, pay attention to your feet and breath, the trees and flowers around you, and everything you see, hear, and feel.

When you're talking to someone, pay attention to every thought that comes to mind. Sift through your feelings, opinions, judgments, and other thoughts, and then let them go. Be present with your actions and actions with you, live in your words, and make a way to your inner self.

Focusing on a person, place, or thing is one way to practice mindfulness meditation. This could be done by making pictures in your mind, relaxing a part of your body, calming your mind, or focusing gently on your breath.

Be aware of your thoughts, words, and actions when you meditate on mindfulness. Don't pay attention to anything that isn't important. Come to this quiet place often and stay there as long as you can.

As a form of self-care, we can do something as simple as look at a flower and let its beauty into our hearts. It could also mean training the mind and heart to be open to the present moment so that our awareness can grow.

The main goal of meditation is to make you feel spiritually connected, mentally clear, emotionally calm, and physically relaxed at the same time.

Aside from mindfulness meditation, there are about 8 other types of meditation, each with its benefits (*Brown, 2021*):

- Focused meditation involves focusing on an internal or external occurrence for an extended period.
- Spiritual meditation is an attempt to develop a connection with a higher power.
- Movement meditation involves gentle movements (such as walking) that guide you into a deeper connection with your body.

The general benefits of meditation in self-care are numerous. Here are a few:

- Helps you become more self-aware
- Helps you notice self-limiting thoughts and quickly change them

- Reduces high blood pressure and alleviates sleep disorders
- Increases imagination and creativity
- Helps alleviate chronic pain and tension headaches

Yoga

Although yoga has undergone a revival in popularity in recent years, it has been around for thousands of years. Yoga's benefits are accessible to anyone of any age and physical ability who is willing to improve their physical and spiritual well-being (*15 Powerful Yoga on YouTube Classes with Black Teachers, 2021*).

Here are a few physical benefits of yoga:

- Increases flexibility
- Helps in weight reduction
- Increases muscle strength and tone

- Improves cardiovascular and circulatory health
- Increases vitality

In addition, the spiritual benefits of yoga are numerous. One of the best benefits of yoga is how it helps individuals effectively deal with stress. Stress can reveal itself in several ways such as back pain, headaches, sleeping pain, addiction, and negative thought cycles. Yoga's incorporation of meditation and breathing techniques can reduce stress levels, improve mental clarity, promote mind relaxation and concentration, and increase calmness.

As much as yoga is vital for self-care, how often have you seen a fellow Black sister stretching on a yoga mat on media? Think back…when last did you see such? Never? That's precisely our predicament. We've been programmed to believe that these self-care acts such as yoga are reserved for a select few. However, but this perception is not true. So, get your yoga mat out and let's begin to connect with your inner self!

Connecting with Nature

As human beings, we are, in fact, an essential part of nature. Spending time with nature connects us to our ancestral origins. Spiritual connection is when we can understand something intuitively that affects our souls and gives our lives meaning. Some people feel spiritually connected when they have a relationship with the Creator, their ancestors, Mother Earth, and all living things. The research shows that being in nature has the biggest effect on the human spirit by giving a sense of connection, vitality, and awe (*10 Physical and Spiritual Benefits of Interacting with Nature, n.d.*).

Creativity

When we express ourselves creatively, we let go of built-in tension and generate a passage of energy from our bodies and into the world. We are essentially translating our stress and trauma into masterpieces. Because we go through emotionally draining adventures every day as Black women, what better way could we care for ourselves than by becoming more creative?

Just for the record, creativity doesn't just mean creating a million-dollar art piece or writing a Grammy-winning song. Creativity could be as small of an act as letting your imagination run wild. First, sit down and ask yourself "What can I achieve if I could never fail?" Then, let your thoughts make themselves known. Next, find fresh and innovative ways to do things in your life. (*Stringfield, 2020*). Break away from the routine and forge a new path for yourself. Now, that's creativity!

Acts of Kindness

We are not just connected to nature but also to each other. And invariably, making others happy will cause you satisfaction. Deliberately caring for others will give us a sense of fulfillment that can only come from the joy we impart to others. Here are suggestions of acts of kindness you can carry out right now.

- Smile. Yes, smile at a stranger, a friend, a loved one...anyone. Just smile. Think back to when someone's face lit up when they saw you approaching. How did you feel? Loved? Exactly!
- Compliment those who cross our paths with sincere words.
- Call that friend or relative whom you love so much and just say how much you appreciate them. Speak your gratitude for their presence in your life.

What 5 spiritual things can you do next week? Don't just think about it, write them down. If possible, journal about how you felt by the end of the week.

For most of this book, we've discussed the importance of self-love. However, self-love is impossible when self-acceptance is absent. In the next chapter, we'll dive deeper into the importance of accepting yourself, your beauty and flaws, your benevolence, and your past. Finally, we'll hash out how you can let go of unhelpful thoughts and negative feelings that deter you from accepting yourself, not how society defines you.

CHAPTER 12: Acceptance - The Final Peace

T his book primarily addresses self-care. However, it's impossible to practice self-care in the absence of self-acceptance. Finally, in this chapter, we shall discuss methods for overcoming destructive mental patterns that prevent you from accepting and loving yourself.

Who Are You?

For a moment, just pause and reflect on this question. If I've never met you (which is most likely true), and throw this question to you, what will be your answer? Would you define yourself by accolades, social circles, bank account balance, or net worth? Or will you tell me about your failures and the not-so-good part of yourself? Most likely, you would opt for the first. This is because, as humans, we would associate ourselves with the positive aspects of our lives. We would promote our positive qualities and ignore the negatives ones as though they never existed.

But what if I took away all those positive characteristics? Would you still love yourself if you were left with only the negative attributes? As I said, defining ourselves by our positives is entirely natural. If you feel the urge to do so, that's fine. However, to truly love yourself, you must have the final piece of the puzzle: acceptance.

Defining Acceptance

According to therapist Russell Grieger, self-acceptance means "you accept that, as a fallible human being, you are less than perfect. As a result, you often perform well, but you will also err at times. Yet, you always and unconditionally accept yourself without judgment."

Self-acceptance is a state where you are completely "cool" with yourself, including your strengths and weaknesses. It means accepting all facets of your life. And by this, it is easy to think self-acceptance means being totally fine with being mediocre. But no, self-acceptance is far from that.

We often think that the only time we should ideally love ourselves is when we've attained specific goals. We subconsciously believe we can self-love only after we've quit that addiction, gotten the new house, and finished the course. We think we are only permitted to unconditionally love ourselves when we have no weakness. Unfortunately, to err is human; our flaws and mistakes prove that we are still human. Suppose we keep on with the mindset mentioned above. In that case, we will live for 70, 80, or 90 years only to discover we never got around to loving ourselves. We will find out that we were only chasing the wind.

The alternative to this, however, is to love ourselves now. Let's associate self-love not with our achievements on the outside but with who we are on the inside. And, by doing so, we extend a hand of grace to our insubstantial self.

The first step to self-improvement is accepting our faults and still loving ourselves. Again, self-love is not a denial of your weaknesses; it means loving yourself (*Bayliss, 2018*). For instance, if you were obese, that's a fact. That's not who you are. But that's a fact about you. Denial of this fact will only lead to further health complications. However, while you accept this fact, you must not fall for the trap of losing your love for the inner you.

In other words, self-acceptance can be said to mean separating yourself from your actions and mistakes. For example, you might have made a mistake at the job, but you are not a failure. You might have lost the contract, but this doesn't mean you are irresponsible. You must not equate your actions to your character. As your faults do not define you.

Look at it this way. We all have that one human that we love. It could be your partner, child, or a long-time friend. Whoever they are, chances are they have great attributes. But also, they will most likely have gotten you annoyed by their actions at some point. I want you to think back to when you got angry with them. Did you judge their character by that singular mistake? You probably didn't. Now, imagine if that human was you. Just like how you keep adoring that beloved person regardless of their past and future errors, this is how you must love yourself unconditionally.

Remember, everyone has made and will make mistakes, including you. However, the first step to self-improvement is accepting and loving yourself, nevertheless.

Letting Go of Guilt

Society has done well to trap us within the snare of guilt because we often do not know what we should feel remorseful about. However, accepting your thoughts and actions becomes easier by understanding what you can do without guilt. Here are some suggestions.

Saying "No"

As previously emphasized, being relied on as a "strong Black woman" has the *onus* of being constantly available to everyone. This should not be your reality, though. As a human, you have the right to say "no" without any explanation given. Of course, the only exception will be when you are bound by a contract, such as within your work hours. However, your free time is yours and totally yours. So don't let anyone make you feel guilty for saying "no". Plus, did I add that no explanation is needed? No is "no." Simple.

Failing

We all have lazy days, don't we? Furthermore, we have all failed at some point. Black excellence was once used with good intent to convey high achievement. But unfortunately, it is now being used harmfully to explain why Blacks must always be successful.

However, humans fail. So, the question is, what do you do when you fail? What do you do when you don't meet your targets? Do you give yourself a hard punch in the gut, or do you hug and support yourself regardless? What's more, with the stereotype around Black excellence, you can easily fall for the compunction trap of not over-achieving. While you should aim for excellence, on days when you miss this target, pick yourself up and try again without shame.

Your Rules

One such instance is not allowing anyone to touch your hair. Do not feel guilty or selfish for not yielding your hair as a servant for their entertainment. When this happens, remember that you are your gatekeeper. No one has a right to access your privacy and heritage (which your hair is, by the way) unless you say otherwise. Your rules are part of who you are. Accept and proclaim them unashamedly!

Being Emotional

You won't always be fine, and on those days, remind yourself that it is okay to not be okay. The "strong Black woman" stereotype has contributed to helping us bottling up our emotions. And on days when we burst into tears, we could see ourselves as less than. Not to say this is entirely our fault. While growing up, we were taught that keeping a solid countenance is the way of the Black community. This façade, unfortunately, is not healthy for your mental health. Hence, whenever you feel emotionally drained and bogged down by the weight of life, remind yourself that it is okay to not be okay.

Your Passion

If you are passionate about a cause, accept your passion. Don't dismiss it because some people are not accepting. Waiting for everyone to be okay with your passion is living your life for others. Telling the unapologetic truth makes others angry, for sure. But people get mad anyway. So, why mind them? Don't stop being passionate, and keep the flame burning, my Nubian Queen!

Forgiveness & Acceptance

What do you consider "good" or "bad"? For example, suppose a negative situation causes you to grow in ways a favorable situation would never have. Would you consider that situation "good"?

You may appreciate that most of your growth came from painful times. It is often said that we don't know how strong we are until strength is our only option, which is so true. Understanding this will help you with acceptance.

But what about forgiveness? Forgiveness means accepting what has happened in the past. This clemency does not mean we condone that act that has been done. Instead, forgiveness is a conscious decision to let go of all the toxic emotions, such as resentment, blame, and anger, we hold onto in dealing with the past circumstances (*Bayliss, 2018*). Thus, mercy is the path to a clearer mind or is an act of mental hygiene. If we refuse to forgive, we are doomed to continuing to punish ourselves for the past hurtful deeds perpetrated by others. By forgiving others, we terminate the pain from the past. And much more, in forgiving others, we learn to forgive ourselves.

Self-forgiveness is crucial to acceptance because we can't move past our mistakes without doing so. Consequently, growth is impossible if we never get up from our falls. As I said, self-forgiveness doesn't mean leaning towards mediocrity. Still, it means choosing to be on your own team as you navigate your vulnerabilities. So, select self-forgiveness today!

Acceptance & Self-Love

There isn't a silver bullet to accepting and loving yourself. This journey requires putting in a daily, conscious effort to raise your head above the waters trying to drown you. Oppositions against your acts of radical self-love will happen. Still, when you consistently apply *P.R.E.S.S.U.R.E*, you can fight back.

P - Practice self-compassion and self-kindness

R - Release beliefs and patterns that no longer serve you (It's terrific to do so)

E - Embrace your uniqueness

S - Speak your truth

S - Surround yourself with friends and relatives who love you for who you are

U - Unapologetically stand up for what you want.

R - Remind yourself of your exceptional qualities; remind yourself you are a Nubian Queen!

E - Envision your future self and make her grateful; remember your past self and make her proud.

As I conclude this chapter, let me tell you a story. Sandra is a long-time friend whom I've known since high school. We were the closest friends, and there was something she hated about herself—her broad nose. That sounds very minor, but to her, the entire universe can see nothing except her broad nose. She became very self-conscious. Coupled with the intersectionality of racism and sexism she faced as she left high school and went on with life, her self-esteem was undermined.

Recently, I had a discussion with her and introduced these concepts of radical self-love to her and guess what? She put the steps into practice (as you will). A few days later, she made a list of the things she really loved about herself (her exceptional qualities) and the things she didn't. She then went further to divide the latter list into what she could change (her bad habit of showing up late for work) and the things she couldn't (her broad nose). She then accepted her flaws while consciously choosing to work on what she could change.

This exercise took less than 20 minutes and provided a much healthier perspective. In addition, the activity boosted Sandra's self-confidence!

This book has many areas of improvement topics and I'm here to assist you to get started on the one you deem to be the most important. Feel free to set up an orientation call with me at https://calendly.com/tabonopublising/orientation-call to explore your options.

CONCLUSION

"You have the power to change perception, to inspire and empower, and to show people how to embrace their complications, and see the flaws, and the true beauty and strength that's inside all of us."

- Beyonce

As women of color in America and the rest of the world, we are both admired and mocked for our strength, beauty, sensuality, and courage. Black girls are subjected to adultification bias. Our teens and women of color are often single mothers who are forced to make it on their own in the world.

Systemic racism and sexism wreak havoc on both our physical and mental health. Everyday energy-draining microaggressions leave us without the strength or time to self-care. Still, holding on to the "strong Black woman" label makes us work even harder when we feel the most tired. But the best way to show how much we love ourselves is to take a step back and practice self-care. As poet Audre Lorde stated, *"Caring for myself is not self-indulgence. It's self-preservation, and that is an act of political warfare."*

This book gave you a completely different view of how you can occupy this society as a Black woman. It shifted the focus to your importance, self-care, and self-love. Self-care means giving yourself all the attention you deserve without permission from anyone because you are a deserving self-loving Nubian Queen!

In this book, you learned that loving yourself is a sign of strength, not selfishness. Self-care is an important, even crucial practice that Black women need to begin as soon as possible. These practices include inner child connection and healing, self-love, emotional self-care, and a spiritual connection. Developing a growth mindset, working on personal growth, harnessing positive affirmations are the steps in this self-care journey. Once accomplished, we start prioritizing our physical and mental needs through diet, exercise, and mindfulness.

No two Black women are the same. So, self-care regiments differ. What we share is the need to overcome a suppressing society in which we are not considered equal. This constant battle causes greater stress, more health problems, and bigger financial obstacles. Consequently, self-care is the ultimate protest to injustice and inequality!

As this book helps you become a better, stronger version of yourself, please show other Black women how to do the same. I hope you enjoyed this experience that reoriented your perspective to transform you into the self-loving Nubian Queen you are predestined to be. Let you, the esteemed Nubian Queen inhabits her space with knowledge of her worth as her birthright. For our self-care is an act of resistance.

From here, I ask that you provide a positive review of this life-changing book. Reviews are essential for authors but more than that, your opinion could be just what other Black women need to locate this book and start working toward that regal life for themselves and their families — it's a sisterhood thing!

Anything worth doing is worth starting poorly!

REFERENCES

Chapter 1

1.   Adeeyo, O. (2022). *Self-Care for Black Women: 150 Ways to Radically Accept & Prioritize Your Mind, Body, & Soul.* Adams Media.
2.   Eltahir, M. (2022, March 15). *Why Self-Love and Self-Care Are Radical for Black Women.* American Urban Radio Networks. *https://aurn.com/why-self-love-and-self-care-are-radical-for-Black-women/*
3.   Frankl, V. E. (1969). *Man's search for meaning an introduction to logotherapy* (14th ed.). Washington Square Press.
4.   Les @ Balanced Black Girl. (2020, August 27). *10 Ways to Practice Self-Love.* Balanced Black Girl. *https://www.balancedBlackgirl.com/practice-self-love/*
5.   Martin, S. L. (2019, May 31). *What is Self-Love and Why Is It So Important?* Psych Central. *https://psychcentral.com/blog/imperfect/2019/05/what-is-self-love-and-why-is-it-so-important*
6.   *On Protecting Black Women.* (n.d.). Retrieved October 31, 2022, from *https://youtu.be/6EIEKe8fVmg*
7.   Walker, S. (2022, September 24). *Self-Love Quiz - Do You Love Yourself Enough?* Empowered and Thriving. *https://empoweredandthriving.com/self-love-quiz/*

Chapter 2

1.   Acquaye. (n.d.). *For Black Women, Self-Care Can be a Radical Act.* OkayAfrica. *https://www.okayafrica.com/Black-women-self-care/*

2. Adeeyo, O. (2022a). *Self-Care for Black Women: 150 Ways to Radically Accept & Prioritize Your Mind, Body, & Soul.* Adams Media.

3. Bergen, J. (2016, September 22). *How to Get in Touch with Your Emotions.* Bergen Counseling Center. *https://www.bergencounselingcenter.com/how-to-get-in-touch-with-your-emotions/*

4. *How Negative Emotions Affect Us.* (2022, February 16). Verywell Mind. *https://www.verywellmind.com/embrace-negative-emotions-4158317*

5. Lorde, A., Keenan, J., & Sanchez, S. (2017). *A Burst of Light: and Other Essays.* Ixia Press.

6. McGill, K. (2022, January 5). *Ten steps to improve your Emotional Self-Awareness using the Emotions and Feelings Wheel.* WordPress.com. *https://drkenmcgill.com/2022/01/05/ten-steps-to-improve-your-emotional-self-awareness-using-the-emotions-and-feelings-wheel/*

7. *Self-Care for the Tolls of Exceptionalism Black Women Face.* (2022, March 2). Verywell Mind. *https://www.verywellmind.com/self-care-for-the-tolls-of-exceptionalism-5219573*

8. support@sitecare.com. (2022, November 2). *Home – HelpGuide.* HelpGuide.org. *https://www.helpguide.org/articles/mental-health/emotional-intelligence-toolkit.html*

Chapter 3

1. *5 effective ways to heal your inner child from adultification trauma.* (2021, October 14). SHETRIBE.

https://www.shetribeconnect.com/post/5-effective-ways-to-heal-your-inner-child-from-adultification-trauma

2. Goldstein, E. (2022, June 6). *What Is An Inner Child | And What Does It Know — Integrative Psychotherapy Mental Health Blog*. Integrative Psychotherapy & Trauma Treatment. *https://integrativepsych.co/new-blog/what-is-an-inner-child*

3. Maté, G., MD, & Ph.D., P. L. A. (2010). *In the Realm of Hungry Ghosts: Close Encounters with Addiction* (Illustrated). North Atlantic Books.

Chapter 4

1. Dowches-Wheeler, J. (2021, October 25). *How to Create Your Own Positive Affirmations for Abundance*. Bright Space Coaching | Leadership Development for Women. *https://www.brightspacecoaching.com/blog/write-your-own-affirmations*

2. Lambersky, S. (2013, October 16). *How to manage your 40,000 negative thoughts a day and keep moving forward*. Financialpost. *https://financialpost.com/entrepreneur/three-techniques-to-manage-40000-negative-thoughts*

3. Les @ Balanced Black Girl. (2021, September 12). *60 Affirmations Every Black Woman Needs to Hear*. Balanced Black Girl. *https://www.balancedBlackgirl.com/10-affirmations-guide-glow-up/*

4. *Using Affirmations: Harnessing Positive Thinking*. (n.d.). Mind Tools. Retrieved November 3, 2022, from

*https://www.mindtools.com/pages/article/affirmations.ht
m*

5. West. (2022, August 8). *100 Empowering Affirmations
    for Black Women Creators and Entrepreneurs.* Our West
    Nest.
    *https://www.ourwestnest.com/blogposts/2021/9/3/empow
    ering-affirmations-for-Black-women*

Chapter 5

1. Cote, C. (2022, March 10). *Growth Mindset vs. Fixed
    Mindset: What's the Difference?* Business Insights
    Blog. *https://online.hbs.edu/blog/post/growth-mindset-
    vs-fixed-mindset*
2. Dweck, C. S. (2007). *Mindset: The New Psychology of
    Success* (Updated Edition). Ballantine Books.
3. Koyenikan, I. (2016). *Wealth for All: Living a Life of
    Success at the Edge of Your Ability.* Grandeur Touch,
    LLC.
4. London Business School. (2018, February 1). *A
    growth mindset helps in coping with expressions of bias.*
    *https://www.london.edu/think/how-a-growth-mindset-
    can-help-in-coping-with-expressions-of-bias-at-work*
5. *MINDSET QUIZ.* (n.d.).
    *https://www.scribbr.com/citation/generator/folders/2DzG
    8V9AgciH0ngIOoghg2/lists/tX8ab4oFM9cJujvM17cnz/c
    ite/webpage/*
6. *Thoughts on the Business of Life.* (n.d.). ForbesQuotes.
    https://www.forbes.com/quotes/7157/
7. Tryumph, D. J. C. (2021, June 15). *How to Develop a
    Growth Mindset.* pan-African. *https://pan-
    african.net/how-to-develop-a-growth-mindset/*

Chapter 6

1. *BOZTEPE: Brain plasticity allows for personal growth.* (n.d.). The Daily Targum. Retrieved November 4, 2022, from *https://dailytargum.com/article/2019/04/brain-plasticity-allows-for-personal-growth*

2. Gamma, E. (2021, March 24). *Brain Plasticity (Neuroplasticity) - Simply Psychology.* *https://www.simplypsychology.org/brain-plasticity.html*

3. *Indeed Career Guide.* (n.d.). *https://www.indeed.com/career-advice/career-development/areas-of-personal-growth*

4. *Negotiating as a Woman of Color.* (2022, January 14). Harvard Business Review. *https://hbr.org/2022/01/negotiating-as-a-woman-of-color*

5. Sasson, R. (2022, October 3). *What Is Personal Growth and Why You Need It.* Success Consciousness | Positive Thinking - Personal Development. *https://www.successconsciousness.com/blog/personal-development/what-is-personal-growth/*

6. *By Denis Waitley The Psychology of Winning: The Ten Qualities of a Total Winner [Audio CD].* (1984). Nightingale Conant.

7. *What Is Neuroplasticity? The Power to Change Your Mind.* (n.d.). Retrieved November 4, 2022, from *https://www.betterup.com/blog/what-is-neuroplasticity*

Chapter 7

1. *A quote by Stephanie Lahart.* (n.d.). Retrieved November 5, 2022, from *https://www.goodreads.com/quotes/7653832-black-girls-beautiful-in-every-shade-and-size-we-ve-got*

2. *Body Image*. (n.d.). National Eating Disorder Collaboration. *https://www.confidentbody.net/uploads/1/7/0/2/17022536/nedc_body_image_fact_sheet.pdf*

3. *Body image - women*. (n.d.). Better Health Channel. Retrieved November 5, 2022, from *https://www.betterhealth.vic.gov.au/health/healthyliving/body-image-women*

4. Brazier, Y. (2022, August 15). *What is body image? https://www.medicalnewstoday.com/articles/249190*

5. Gasperino, J. (1996). Ethnic differences in body composition and their relation to health and disease in women. *Ethnicity &Amp; Health, 1*(4), 337–347. *https://doi.org/10.1080/13557858.1996.9961803*

6. Poetry Foundation. (1994). *Still I Rise by Maya Angelou*. *https://www.poetryfoundation.org/poems/46446/still-i-rise*

7. Wikipedia contributors. (2022a, October 21). List of ethnic groups of Africa. Wikipedia. *https://en.wikipedia.org/wiki/List_of_ethnic_groups_of_Africa*

8. Wikipedia contributors. (2022b, October 15). *Bantu peoples of South Africa*. Wikipedia. *https://en.wikipedia.org/wiki/Bantu_peoples_of_South_Africa*

9. Wikipedia contributors. (2022c, August 22). *Cushitic speaking peoples*. Wikipedia. *https://en.wikipedia.org/wiki/Cushitic_speaking_peoples*

10. Wikipedia contributors. (2022d, September 25). *Nilotic peoples*. Wikipedia. *https://en.wikipedia.org/wiki/Nilotic_peoples*

11. Wikipedia contributors. (2022e, October 16). *Pygmy peoples*. Wikipedia. https://en.wikipedia.org/wiki/Pygmy_peoples

Chapter 8

1. *25 Quick Ways to Reduce Stress*. (2018, October 10). Colorado Law. https://www.colorado.edu/law/25-quick-ways-reduce-stress
2. Bondy, H. (2019, August 21). *Nutritionist Maya Feller's 5 best health tips for women of color*. MSNBC.com. https://www.msnbc.com/know-your-value/nutritionist-maya-feller-s-5-best-health-tips-women-color-n1044061
3. *CDC Newsroom*. (2016, January 1). CDC. https://www.cdc.gov/media/releases/2016/p0215-enough-sleep.html
4. *Heart Disease Risk: How Race and Ethnicity Play a Role*. (n.d.). Cleveland Clinic. Retrieved November 5, 2022, from https://my.clevelandclinic.org/health/articles/23051-ethnicity-and-heart-disease
5. Holland, B. M. A. S. (2021, November 24). *Nine Badass Black Women Who Are Changing the Workout Game*. The Root. https://www.theroot.com/nine-badass-black-women-who-are-changing-the-workout-ga-1846113017
6. Johnson, D. (2019). Are Sleep Patterns Influenced by Race/Ethnicity – a Marker of Relative Advantage or Disadvantage? Evidence to Date. *Nat Sci Sleep*, 2019(11), PMC6664254. https://doi.org/10.2147/NSS.S169312
7. Miller, S. S. (2022, June 6). *Obesity Among Black Women: Fighting the Disease Through Community*.

HealthyWomen. *https://www.healthywomen.org/condition/obesity-among-black-women*

8. Qfrog Labs. (2020, November 24). *How Can Honey Help You Battle Depression?* Eiwa Honey. *https://eiwahoney.in/blogs/honey-and-health/how-can-honey-help-you-battle-depression*

9. Thompson, D. (2022, June 2). *Study: Black Women Lose Less Weight Than White Women on Same Diet.* Consumer Health News | HealthDay. *https://consumer.healthday.com/vitamins-and-nutrition-information-27/dieting-to-lose-weight-health-news-195/study-black-women-lose-less-weight-than-white-women-on-same-diet-683243.html*

10. *Your body is precious. It is our vehicle for awakening. Treat it with care.* (2014, July 23). Tiny Buddha. *https://tinybuddha.com/wisdom-quotes/your-body-is-precious-it-is-our-vehicle-for-awakening-treat-it-with-care/*

Chapter 9

1. The Audre Lorde Project (n.d.). *Breaking Isolation: Self Care and Community Care Tools for Our People.* Retrieved September 12, 2022, from https://alp.org/breaking-isolation-self-care-and-community-care-tools-our-people

2. Brooten-Brooks, M. (2022, January 24). *What Is Boundary Setting? A guide to setting limits with Parents, Partners, Friends, and Co-Workers.* Retrieved September 12, 2022, from *https://www.verywellhealth.com/setting-boundaries-5208802*

3. Chesak, J. (2018, December 10). *The No BS Guide to Protecting Your Emotional Space.* Retrieved September 12, 2022, from *https://www.healthline.com/health/mental-health/set-boundaries#intro*

4. Bashford, S. (2022, May 26). *How to know your worth (and discover your true values).* Psychologies. Retrieved September 12, 2022, from https://www.psychologies.co.uk/how-to-know-your-worth/

5. Cuzzone, K. (2021, February 5). *20 Organizations That Support Black Women During Black History Month and Beyond.* PureWow. Retrieved September 12, 2022, from https://www.purewow.com/wellness/organizations-that-support-Black-women

6. Candelario, C (2021, February 8). *21 Mental Health Resources for BIPOC (and 5 Tips to Finding the Right Therapist for You).* PureWow. Retrieved September 12, 2022, from https://www.purewow.com/wellness/bipoc-mental-health-resources

Chapter 10

1. Davenport, D. (2022, February 9). *Best Advice Ever: Raising a Proud Emotionally Healthy Black*

Child. Creating a Family.
https://creatingafamily.org/adoption-
category/best-advice-ever-raising-emotionally-
healthy-black-child/

2. Dewar, G. (2022, April 21). *Teaching empathy: Evidence-based tips for fostering empathic awareness in children.* PARENTING SCIENCE.
https://parentingscience.com/teaching-empathy-tips/

3. *How to Teach Your Kids to Love the Skin They're In.* (2018, June 24). Are Those Your Kids.
https://arethoseyourkids.com/teaching-kidslove-skin/

4. *Moving "The Talk" to "The Walk" for Black Children.* (2021, December 16). EmbraceRace.
https://www.embracerace.org/resources/moving-the-talk-to-the-walk-for-black-children

Chapter 11
1. *10 Physical and Spiritual Benefits of Interacting with Nature | Blog.* (n.d.). Elite World Hotels. Retrieved November 6, 2022, from
https://www.eliteworldhotels.com.tr/blog-en/10-physical-and-spiritual-benefits-of-interacting-with-nature.1249.aspx

2. *15 Powerful Yoga On Youtube Classes With Black Teachers.* (2021, September 29). Wellness Travel Diaries. *https://wellnesstraveldiaries.com/yoga-on-youtube/*

3. *Attention Required! | Cloudflare.* (n.d.). Retrieved November 6, 2022, from

https://www.amanet.org/articles/how-to-say-no-assertively/

4. Brown, K. (2021, December 12). *Why Black Women Need to Meditate and How to Get Started*. Black Girl Nerds. *https://Blackgirlnerds.com/why-Black-women-need-to-meditate-and-how-to-get-started/*

5. Haven Inspired. (2021, February 14). *7 minute guided meditation for BLACK WOMEN*. YouTube. *https://www.youtube.com/watch?v=VDK5VL0N3RQ*

6. *Just a moment. . .* (n.d.). Retrieved November 6, 2022, from *https://healthyspirituality.org/the-spiritual-practice-of-kindness/*

7. *Meditation and Mindfulness; What's the Difference?* (n.d.). Gaia. Retrieved November 6, 2022, from *https://www.gaia.com/article/meditation-vs-mindfulness-methods-mindsets-for-lasting-peace?gclid=Cj0KCQjwwfiaBhC7ARIsAGvcPe7mKqeEN3MgydLhIkqy3rez2O-fF_DBT3eJl2Nos7chX1BnzDUHHGYaAlPfEALw_wcB*

8. Profile », B. K. R. V. (n.d.). *Jessamyn Stanley on Challenging the Whiteness of Wellness*. Bitch Media. Retrieved November 6, 2022, from *https://www.bitchmedia.org/article/jessamyn-stanley-black-women-microaggressions-wellness-yoga*

9. Sagelife Senior Living. (2021, September 9). *The Health Benefits Of Spirituality*. SageLife.com. *https://www.sagelife.com/resources/the-health-benefits-of-spirituality/*

10. Stringfield, R. (2020, July 14). *How Being Creative Helps Black People Find Their Mind/Body Connection*. Greatist. *https://greatist.com/discover/creativity-as-healing-comfort-and-joy*

11. Todorov, G. (2022, November 1). *How to promote your blog*. Learn Digital Marketing. *https://thrivemyway.com/how-to-be-more-creative/*

12. *What Is Spirituality?* (n.d.). Taking Charge of Your Health & Wellbeing. Retrieved November 6, 2022, from *https://www.takingcharge.csh.umn.edu/what-spirituality*

13. Williamson, M. (n.d.). *Spirituality*. https://Top 500 Marianne Williamson Quotes (2022 Update) - Quotefancy *https://quotefancy.com/marianne-williamson-quotes*

Chapter 12

1. Bayliss, N. (2018, April 5). *The Importance of Acceptance & Forgiveness*. Nicole Bayliss. *https://nicolebayliss.com.au/importance-acceptance-forgiveness/*

2. Ira, P. (2022, June 27). *5 Things You Should Stop Making Black Women Feel Guilty For*. Medium. *https://aninjusticemag.com/5-things-you-should-stop-making-Black-women-feel-guilty-for-582dd8b6646*

3. Team, O. M. (2021, May 22). *26 Nathaniel Branden Quotes On Success In Life –*. OverallMotivation. *https://www.overallmotivation.com/quotes/nathaniel-branden-quotes/*

4. Team, T. (2021, July 12). *The Skin I'm In: Practicing Radical Self-Acceptance*. Therapy for Black Girls. *https://therapyforblackgirls.com/2021/07/12/the-skin-im-in-practicing-radical-self-acceptance/*

Conclusion

1. Phelps, N. (2016, June 7). *Beyoncé Is the CFDA's Fashion Icon, Read Her Speech.* Vogue./ *https://www.vogue.com/article/beyonce-cfda-fashion-icon-speech*

ABOUT THE AUTHOR

Patsy Clarke came to the United States from Jamaica when she was just a child. She made the decision to invest in her education, and today she is an engineer who lives in South Florida. She is a single mother who recognizes the importance of setting a positive example for her child and makes every effort to do so. She has written a number of books, one of which is entitled "Positive Affirmations for the Black Child."

Patsy, a self-assured Black woman who was bolstered by a caring sisterhood, succeeded in forging a path for herself as a proud single mother. It is essential to one's happiness and success to have meaningful social support while also loving oneself.